GROWING
WITH NATURE

A YEAR OF PLAY, CREATIVITY,
RITUALS AND MINDFULNESS
FOLLOWING THE RHYTHM OF NATURE

LIDIA SCOTTO DI VETTA

Paperback 978-0-6459313-0-3
eBook 978-0-6459313-9-6

First published in 2023

Wise Nature Publishing
Gubbi Gubbi/Kabi Kabi Country, Sunshine Coast, Australia

Big Scrub Nature Play
www.bigscrubnatureplay.com

For Lorenzo and Allegra,
my everyday sunshine.

CONTENTS

INTRODUCTION

08   Growing with nature
10   About me
12   How to use this book

JANUARY

17   New beginnings
19   Welcome the new year
22   Earth Magic: Rosemary
26   Full Moon: Make a dream pillow
29   Nature Play: Summer treasure hunt +
Painting with rosemary ink + A seaside adventure
36   Storytelling: Spinnie and the ocean

FEBRUARY

40   Opening up to Mother Earth's bounty
41   Earth Magic: Basil
49   Full Moon: Smudge sticks
52   In the Kitchen: Make traditional pesto
55   Nature Play: Mortar and pestle sensory play
57   End of summer campfire

MARCH

63   Planting seeds of kindness
64   Earth Magic: Broad-leaved paperbark tree
68   Full Moon: Sand painting
70   In the Kitchen: Cooking with paperbark
72   Nature Play: Paperbark nature journal +
Making natural paint + Earth pigments
79   Mindfulness: Seeds of kindness cards

APRIL

84   Grounding, connecting with the Earth
85   Earth Magic: Clay
88   Full Moon: Moon phases garland
90   In the Kitchen: Apples
93   Nature Play: A guide to working with clay
104 Storytelling: The clay gnomes
106 Mindfulness: Listening clay

MAY

110 Warming our senses
112 Earth Magic: Bees
121 Full Moon: Hand rolled beeswax candles
123 In the Kitchen: Honey cake
124 Nature Play: Here is the beehive + Wildflowers seed bombs + Catching autumn colours + Beeswax leaves + Leaf rubbing + Autumn leaves games
135 Mindfulness: Bee breathing

JUNE

138 Shine your inner light
140 Earth Magic: Winter Solstice
144 The importance of rituals
150 Bring the magic of the solstice into your home
154 In the Kitchen: Make sun bread
156 Nature Play: Solstice lanterns + Taking care of others + Giving back to nature
164 Mindfulness: Finding stillness - sit spot

JULY

167 A journey home
169 Earth Magic: Banksias
176 Full Moon: Make a boomerang
180 Nature Play: Adopt a tree + Make your own adventure binoculars + Story stones
185 Humpback whales
190 Storytelling: The white whale

AUGUST

195 Joyful transitions
197 Earth Magic: Wattles
200 Full Moon: Moon water
202 In the Kitchen: Cooking with wattleseed
206 Nature Play: Painting wattles + Nature perfume + Dyeing with wattles + Wattle crowns + Felt wattles
216 Storytelling: The wattle fairies

SEPTEMBER

219 Gentle whisperings of life stirring
221 Signs of spring
228 Earth Magic: Australian Magpies
232 Full Moon: Moon breathing
233 In the Kitchen: A spring cleansing ritual
238 Nature Play: Build a nest + The secret language of birds + Bird shapes
242 Storytelling: A nest for mama magpie

OCTOBER

246 Find your wings
248 Earth Magic: Butterfly migration
251 Full Moon: Follow the journey of the Moon with a phenology wheel
256 In the Kitchen: A spring picnic
262 Nature Play: Make a butterfly feeder

NOVEMBER

270 The grounding energy of rocks
272 Earth Magic: Rocks
274 Full Moon: Full moon magic potion
276 In the Kitchen: Let's make stone soup
279 Nature Play: Playing with stones
287 Mindfulness: World Kindness Day + Kindness rocks

DECEMBER

291 Welcome Summer
293 Earth Magic: Dandelions
298 Summer solstice magic
300 Full Moon: Dandelion honey
302 In the Kitchen: Happy Summer tea
304 Nature Play: Dandelion pouch + Wildflower playdough + Midsummer wand + Plants ID cards
311 Mindfulness: The wise dandelion

CONCLUSION

313 Conclusion
314 Resources + References
315 Thank yous

INTRODUCTION

GROWING WITH NATURE

"Every child is born a naturalist. His eyes are, by nature, open to the glories of the stars, the beauty of the flowers, and the mystery of life". – R. Search

There was a time when people lived in harmony with nature and in sync with the intricate life cycles of plants, animals, and insects. They eagerly anticipated and celebrated the flowering and fruiting times of important food and medicinal plants, the movement of birds, the timing of animal breeding, the shift of winds, and the moon cycles.

This knowledge was considered sacred, and was preserved through storytelling, songs, dance, and ceremonies. It was a time when the boundary between humankind and the natural world was blissfully blurred... nearly invisible.

From where we stand now, this deep, intimate relationship with nature may seem like an elusive dream, a nostalgic and unattainable notion, maybe even impractical. Still, every so often, a flicker of that ancient connection reawakens within us. We sense it in the peaceful solitude of a long bush walk, or the soothing embrace of the ocean. We find it in the raw, primal pleasure of digging our hands in soil, harvesting food we have grown and tended to with love and dedication. We rediscover a lost sense of delight and playfulness as we marvel at the coming and going of birds in our backyards.

But the most astonishing awakening of all occurs when a child enters our lives. Through their pure eyes, we begin to see nature differently. Everything is infused with awe and wonder, and a sense of possibility.

Listening to the leaves rustling in the breeze becomes a soothing experience. Playing barefoot on the grass invites us to move with awareness. Natural resources such as pine cones, grass, rocks, leaves, rain, spider webs, sticks, seashells, pebbles, and dirt provide endless opportunities for play and imagination.

It is clear that children are innately connected to nature and it is our job as parents and educators to nurture that relationship - not only in the early years, but throughout their lives.

What if nature became more than just a backdrop for recreation, but instead, a wise teacher we invited into our homes? And what if we embarked on this journey of exploration and discovery alongside our children?

If deep inside you there is a longing - to slow down, to choose presence instead of busyness, to walk this Earth wide-eyed and open-hearted - then this book is for you.

No matter who and where you are on this beautiful planet, nature will gently lead you into the precious work of unfolding, healing and grounding you, if you allow it to. And like a pebble dropped into a tranquil lake, it will create ripples in our children's lives.

ABOUT ME

I grew up in a small coastal town in the south of Italy with my parents, siblings, and a large extended family. When I think of my childhood, I can almost taste the sea. I can feel the familiar tangles in my salt-encrusted hair and the gritty sand forever in my toes, trapped in the plastic sandals my mother forced me to wear for years. The beach and the sea, the cliffs and the rockpools were my playground, and the only place where I could spend hours roaming free, fully immersed in play.

Although we lived in a small apartment, nature was at the core of important rituals and traditions in our family. Each year, we anticipated the bounty of juicy tomatoes, sweet figs and wine grapes and the big gatherings that came with the harvesting and preserving of these treasures. We celebrated midsummer with a midnight swim and welcomed the day with the comforting smell of fresh bread in the kitchen. My grandfathers taught me to understand and protect the land and the sea. From my grandmothers I learnt the ways in which plants can heal us, inside and outside.

Of course, I did not understand any of this while I was young – living carefree and dreaming of big cities and exotic places around the world. It was only when I gazed into the eyes of my first child that everything started to fall into place. I relived my childhood through those eyes and felt like the jigsaw pieces of my life were finally fitting together. A re-awakening and, perhaps, a surrendering – to something that was way bigger than me – began to unfold. Nature became my spiritual home, my gateway to the divine.

When I became a mother, I knew I wanted my children to grow with an understanding that we are all part of this universe, interconnected in this amazing web of life. That trees and plants hold ancient wisdom, that animals are friends with many gifts to share, that the moon and the stars can reveal secrets sometimes too big for us to comprehend.

And so, soon after the arrival of my second child, I found myself on the path of becoming a Forest school leader and in 2019 we created Big Scrub Nature Play.

I say we because it was truly a joint venture – my children were (and still are) the driving force behind it, helping and inspiring me in every way.

Today, thanks to Big Scrub, I have the opportunity to share my love for nature play and nature pedagogy – connecting to hundreds of families through our programs, and supporting schools and homeschooling communities implementing experiential, nature-based curriculums.

Many of the stories, crafts and activities you will find in this book have been created, tried and tested on countless adventures with my own two wildlings and all the children I am so blessed to spend time with. Whenever I can, I draw on the wisdom of the traditional custodians of this land, Aboriginal and Torres Strait Islander peoples, whose knowledge and connection to land continues to be a source of awe and inspiration for me.

Nature is filled with magic and this book is about finding, and recognising that magic. I hope it will guide you and your child to a place of discovery, connection and wonder.

Find ways to be joyful in nature.
Let yourself and your child fall in love with it.

HOW TO USE THIS BOOK

Australia's vast expanse makes the conventional Western four season calendar, which divides the year into four roughly equal sequential phases (summer, autumn, winter, spring), greatly ineffective for encapsulating our country's diverse weather and climate. Unlike this conventional approach, Aboriginal and Torres Strait Islander communities have long possessed a deep understanding of the seasons and their transitions by observing local flora and fauna, weather patterns, fire activity, and even the stars.

In this book, I follow the seasons and rhythms of the eastern coast of Australia, specifically across the regions where I live – Bundjalung Country, the area known today as the Northern Rivers in New South Wales, and Gubbi Gubbi Country, also known as the Sunshine Coast in South East Queensland. It is the result of countless hours immersed in exploration and play across beautiful beaches, lakes, rivers, creeks, mountains and rainforests. Or just sitting in my own garden, watching what is blooming or ready to harvest, and the dance of birds and insects as they go about their day.

Simply put, it is based on my observation of the natural world around *me*. While you may notice some similarities, the number of seasons, the length of each season, and the changes they bring in nature can greatly differ based on your location. I hope this book will become a source of inspiration for further and deeper observation of the natural world around *you*.

Within each chapter, you will find ways to invite the wonders of nature into your home and playtime through the following categories:

Earth Magic
Plant and animal allies that will guide us in our explorations

In the Kitchen
Nourishing recipes to create with love and mindful presence

Full Moon
Special activities and celebrations to harness the energy of lunar cycles

Nature Play
Outdoor adventures and crafts that spark imagination and curiosity

Stories and Mindfulness
Inspiring tales and nature-based mindfulness prompts to instil a sense of presence and gratitude

All the activities have been simplified to allow children to actively participate and create alongside you. They can, however, be easily adapted to different ages and abilities, allowing you to explore these themes year after year, and watch your child grow with them.

More than a set of instructions, think of them as prompts to create moments of connection in your home. Let your children be your guides. Allow them to take the lead, and be ready to be amazed.

A DIFFERENT APPROACH

In a world awash with information, children are often inundated with knowledge. Yet, too rarely are they invited to venture outside and given the time to linger, to experience, and to fall in love with the very things they are taught through textbooks, videos, and digital apps.

At the same time, many environmental groups and nature-based programs foster a 'look, but don't touch' mentality. Don't step off the trails, don't pick the flowers, don't touch the worms, don't climb the trees. In an effort to protect nature, we put it behind glass.

To me, nature connection is a felt experience. It is sight and sound, smell and taste, touch, and elements of mystery, or magic, all coming together. My approach – inspired by nature connection advocates like Rachel Carson and Joseph Cornell, and guided by the ethos of the Forest school movement – advocates for a full sensory immersion and a commitment to a head, hearts and hands model for transformational learning.

In the course of our programs, children are not only allowed but encouraged to revel in Mother Earth's embrace – to play in and with nature; to build shelters and climb trees; light fires; pick fruits, flowers and seedpods; to gently collect pieces of bark and, safely get up close to animals. We tread this path with respect and compassion, leaving no trace and are conscious that we share that space, that tree, that flower meadow with hundreds, if not thousands of other creatures. With this approach the emphasis is equally inward and outward.

Throughout the pages of this book, I will repeatedly encourage you to venture outside and forage, collect, harvest, and pick. Touch nature, smell it, feel it, and sink your hands in it. Do it responsibly and with a generous heart.

When collecting flowers the rule of thumb is "one for me, five for the bee". Sticks, leaves and seed pods can always be collected from the ground. Before taking from a tree, establish a connection, ask for permission. Touch the tree and tune into your heart – you will find the answer within you.

Always, always give thanks – make an offering, hug the tree, sing to it.

These values, and this profound connection, form the foundation of Growing with Nature.

SCAN THIS QR CODE WITH YOUR PHONE TO TAKE YOU TO BIGSCRUBNATUREPLAY.COM WHERE YOU WILL FIND HELPFUL VIDEO DEMONSTRATIONS FOR SOME OF THE ACTIVITIES IN THIS BOOK, PLUS ALL THE PRINTABLE TEMPLATES AND A FEW LITTLE EXTRA GOODIES, TOO.

JANUARY

NEW BEGINNINGS

Salty skin, bare feet, deep breaths, low tide magic, thunderstorms lighting up the night sky, afternoon naps in the shade of a tree, the soothing buzz of cicadas singing. Summer is in full swing, and we welcome a new year.

The bright flowers of the pigface (*Carpobrotus virescens*) dot the sand dunes. When the fruiting body swells up and turns deep red, it is ready to eat – a sweet and salty treat. Native raspberries and blackberries are flowering and fruiting, a delicious snack for when we are out on long bush walks. Reptiles are active and enjoying the heat.

With the Sun shining at its brightest, we are gifted with endless opportunities to be outdoors. Let us seize the magic of summer.

"TOMORROW IS THE FIRST BLANK PAGE OF A 365 PAGE BOOK. WRITE A GOOD ONE." - B.PAISLEY

WELCOME THE NEW YEAR

Our children may not yet fully grasp the concept of time (and let's be honest, do any of us really?), but the idea of a new year, a fresh start, and celebrating life is something that resonates and fills us with joy. As the year draws to a close, we have a wonderful opportunity to create meaningful rituals and traditions that are unique to our family. Here are some ideas to help you welcome the new year with open hearts, gratitude, and a shared vision for the future.

FAREWELL WITH LOVE AND APPRECIATION

Gather your family in a cosy circle, whether on a mat or around the table, and invite each person to share their favourite moments of the past year. Take the time to revisit special occasions, holidays, and personal milestones, savouring these cherished memories with hearts full of gratitude.

For young children who may need a little help recalling past events, consider printing out a selection of photos capturing precious family moments or creating a slideshow to play on your computer or TV. Laugh, wonder, shed happy tears, and express heartfelt appreciation together as you relive these special times.

USE NATURE TO RELEASE WHAT NO LONGER SERVES YOU

Too often, we carry burdens that weigh us down unnecessarily, whether it be exhaustion, fear, clutter, or challenging experiences. As we enter the new year it's time to create space for fresh opportunities by leaving behind what no longer serves us. Here are some beautiful rituals using nature's elements to help release these emotions and make way for a fresh start.

FIRE

Gather your family and ask each member to write down or draw on small pieces of paper what they are ready to let go of. Find a safe space- such as a fire pit, fireplace, or even light a candle, to burn these papers.

Engage your senses as you witness the flames taking hold of the paper, symbolising the release of whatever no longer serves you. Let the fire carry away these burdens, making space for new beginnings.

WATER

Just as fire transforms burdens into ashes, water has the power to cleanse and wash them away. If water is your element, consider incorporating it into your ritual. Take a dip in the ocean, a nearby lake, or even enjoy a bath together as a family. Make it joyful and playful by jumping into the water hand in hand, splashing each other, and symbolically washing away what you no longer wish to carry into the new year. Allow the water to refresh and renew, leaving you feeling lighter and ready for new adventures.

CREATE A SENSE OF ANTICIPATION

What is everyone looking forward to in the new year? Creating a family vision board can be a wonderful way to connect with each other and share dreams and aspirations.

Provide magazines, colourful markers, glue, and a large sheet of paper or a poster board. Invite each family member to find images or words that represent their dreams and goals for the upcoming year. Cut and paste, write, draw, make it as unique as you are!

Maybe you want to visit a new country or spend more time in nature together. Play board games after dinner. Have special one-on-one time with each of your children every day. Or it might be something you'd like to do for your community or the environment. Dream big, but don't forget that magic often lies in simple things.

And finally... Take a moment to lavish yourself with self-love and appreciation for all the things you've done right this year. Forgive yourself for the times you missed the mark. Express gratitude for all the large and small miracles in your life. Open your heart to receiving more in the coming year. Embrace the beauty of the present moment and treasure the memories you create together as you embark on another journey around the Sun!

EARTH MAGIC

ROSEMARY

As the Sun reaches its highest point in the sky, nature bursts with vibrant energy, making it the perfect time to harvest plants for your family medicinal cabinet. This month, let's embark on an exciting journey of discovery as we connect with *Rosmarinus officinalis*, or rosemary, a plant for magic and protection.

Rosemary, an aromatic evergreen shrub, has been held in high regard by civilisations throughout history. Its significance reaches far and wide.

Rosemary is closely associated with the Greek goddess Aphrodite, who represents beauty, fertility, and love. Legend has it that Aphrodite was born from the foam of the Mediterranean Sea, where this plant thrives – drawing sustenance from the moist sea air carried by the breeze. The name Rosmarinus, in fact, is derived from the Latin words "ros" meaning 'dew' and "marinus" meaning 'of the sea'.

Rosemary was so highly regarded that it was burned as incense in temples and used as a fragrance by queens, goddesses, and brides. For centuries, this plant has been cherished and revered for its remarkable antiseptic and disinfecting properties.

But its wonders don't stop there. Did you know that rosemary is also linked to the power of remembrance? Its aroma is believed to boost memory and mental clarity. Imagine that — a plant that not only brings healing but also helps us remember important things in our lives.

In the realm of herbal lore, rosemary holds a special place as a plant associated with magic and protection.

Governed by the element fire and the Sun, rosemary embodies the energy of warmth, vitality, and creativity. It has the power to ignite our hearts and unleash our creative spirit.

Rosemary attracts faerie and good energies, and offers protection for your home. It acts as a guardian, shielding your space from negative influences. What better way to start a new year than connecting with this wonderful plant.

To fully harness the energy of rosemary, keep a sprig of this magical herb in your rooms or even grow it in your garden. Position it in a sunny spot near a door or window - the aroma of rosemary will permeate your surroundings, creating an atmosphere of tranquillity and positive energy.

ROSEMARY MIST

Rosemary mist offers a delightful and natural way to nourish your hair, leaving it soft, shiny, and promoting healthy growth. Children love making this infusion – let them pick the fresh rosemary and ask them to help you separate the leaves from the woody stem.

Keep a bottle of rosemary mist next to your child's hairbrush in the bathroom. You can also use it as part of your bedtime ritual – spray on your child's hair and gently brush it before going to bed. A soothing practice that will help your child drift off to a peaceful sleep.

Things to gather:

- fresh rosemary sprigs
- water
- a spray bottle

Directions. Begin by placing the fresh rosemary sprigs at the bottom of a stockpot. Cover them with 2 cups of water.

Bring the water to a boil, then reduce the heat. Cover the pot with a lid, and allow to simmer for approximately 1 hour. Stir occasionally during this time. You will notice that the water will take on a dark brown colour as the rosemary infuses.

Once the simmering is complete, strain the rosemary infused water and set it aside to cool until it reaches a safe temperature to handle. Transfer into a glass spray bottle, ready for use on wet hair. There's no need to rinse it out.

Storage. To ensure the longevity of your rosemary mist, store it in the refrigerator or in a cool, dark cabinet.

SUNSHINE TEA

Whether you choose to enjoy it during a peaceful moment alone or share it with loved ones, this refreshing and invigorating infusion will surely bring a touch of brightness to your day. Equally delicious warm or chilled over ice.

Ingredients:

- fresh rosemary
- water
- lemon rind
- honey (optional)

Method. Add fresh rosemary and lemon rind to a cup. Pour boiling water over them, ensuring the ingredients are fully submerged. Allow the mixture to steep for a minimum of 15 minutes. Squeeze some fresh lemon juice into the tea to enhance the citrus notes. Add a touch of honey, if desired.

Strain the mixture and enjoy!

FULL MOON

MAKE A DREAM PILLOW

As the days stretch long and are vibrant with energy, bedtime may sometimes be a bit later than usual for our little ones. To support their relaxation and ensure restorative sleep, this month we will create dream pillows filled with sacred herbs.

As we delve into this enchanting craft, we invoke the power and energy of the full moon as a reminder of the natural rhythms of the universe and the harmony we can find in aligning with its energies.

Children love snuggling up with their dream pillows, and the soothing aroma of the herbs will bring a sense of comfort and security to their sleep. Sweet dreams!

Things to gather:

dried herbs of your choice
a large bowl for mixing
a muslin string bag or fabric for sewing your own bag
sewing supplies

Herbs to promote peaceful sleep

- Rosemary
- Lavender
- Chamomile
- Hops
- Passionflower
- Lemon balm

Herbs to promote vivid dreams and/ or a meditative state

(recommended for adults only)

- Sage
- Mugwort
- Tulsi
- Rose

Directions. Begin by creating a blend of dried herbs you find soothing and calming. Once you have selected your desired herbs, let your child pour and mix them together into a large bowl.

Take a moment to inhale their fragrance together. Using a spoon, carefully scoop your herb mixture into a small muslin string bag or you can sew your own pouch using cotton fabric or wool felt. To make it extra special, you can embroider your child's name or initials on the bag.

Be sure to secure the bag tightly to prevent the herbs from spilling out.

While working on your dream pillow, you may choose to offer a prayer, inviting positive energy and intentions to surround the sleep experience of your child. Your tranquillity and mindful presence will channel your love and care into this special creation.

Dream pillows make a thoughtful gift, and are usually loved and appreciated by children and adults alike.

Why not make one for yourself, too?

READY TO MAKE ONE?
FOLLOW THE STEP-BY-STEP
VIDEO INSTRUCTIONS ON
OUR WEBSITE

NATURE PLAY

A SUMMER HUNT

Enjoy looking for signs of summer. Prepare a picnic bag, gather your loved ones, and set off on a nature walk. If you have binoculars or a magnifying glass, bring them along. Before you begin, print out the treasure hunt list provided (either by photocopying the page or printing from our website) and challenge yourselves to find as many of these nature items as possible.

Summer is for slowing down, connecting and celebrating. Once your treasure hunt comes to an end, find a peaceful spot to lay down your picnic blanket. Take a moment to relax and savour the rewards of your adventure. Indulge in a cup of Sunshine tea or hot cocoa together. Close your eyes and feel the sun on your skin.

These precious memories will warm your heart long after summer fades away.

NATURE TREASURE HUNT

Peek under stones or high up in trees. Hiding around us is a world of treasures, waiting to be seen.

Can you find everything on this list?

☐ A DANDELION

☐ A BUTTERFLY

☐ A BUG OR INSECT

☐ THREE LEAVES OF DIFFERENT SHAPES

☐ A FEATHER

☐ A CATERPILLAR

☐ A FUNNY SHAPED CLOUD

☐ A PIECE OF BARK

☐ A SPIDER WEB

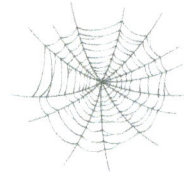

☐ AN INTACT SEASHELL

"What our lives lack most is wonder. To meet those who still marvel at nothing, at a butterfly, at the driving rain, at a poppy, at the song of a bird. Almost nothing. So much. So many little things, humble little treasures."

Jacques Dor

PAINTING WITH ROSEMARY INK

Creating botanical inks is a captivating way to deepen our connection with nature while exploring our artistic side. The possibilities are truly endless, as we can make inks from various plants, flowers, seeds, berries, and bark.

Let's begin with a simple recipe using the aromatic rosemary to achieve a beautiful earthy brown hue.

Things to gather:

fresh rosemary
water
dried whole cloves or wintergreen oil
watercolour paper

Directions. In a stainless steel pot, place the fresh rosemary and add enough water to cover the surface of the plant material. As a general guideline, use 2 cups of water for every cup of plant material.

Bring the water to a boil, then add 2 tablespoons of white vinegar and 1 tablespoon of salt. Let the mixture boil for a few more minutes, then reduce the heat to a simmer.

Stir occasionally and let it simmer for 3-4 hours – this will help extract the colour from the plant. Be patient, as achieving a rich and deep-coloured ink will require a few hours of supervised reduction.

Once the plant has gifted all its colours, remove the pot from the heat and let the mixture cool completely. Filter the plant material using a fine mesh strainer or a muslin cloth and pour the filtered ink into a sterilised jar.

Now it's time to let your creativity flourish! Let the earthy hue of rosemary inspire and guide you. Use the next page to test your botanical ink or use on thick watercolour paper.

Storage. Add a clove or a drop of wintergreen oil to your jar – these natural additives will help prolong the shelf life of the ink, allowing you to enjoy its vibrancy for a longer period.

MY BOTANICAL INKS

Made with _____ and love

by _____

A SEASIDE ADVENTURE

Grab a bucket and get ready to explore the treasures hiding in our sandy shores. Start by collecting and gathering seashells in as many different shapes and sizes as you can find. Take a moment to taste the saltiness of the ocean air, filling your senses with the essence of the sea. Feel the soft sand beneath your toes and the gentle touch of the sun's rays on your skin.

TRACING SEASHELLS

Find a large piece of paper, spread it out, and carefully arrange your seashell collection beside it. One by one, trace the outlines of each seashell onto the paper, capturing their unique shapes and intricate details. Imagine the journey these shells have taken, carried by the tides, and deposited on the shore for you to discover.

Use your imagination to create a simple story to share with your child.

STORYTELLING

SPINNIE AND THE OCEAN

Once upon a time, on a beautiful Australian beach, a little spinifex named Spinnie dared to follow her heart's calling.

Spinnie's home was on the white sand dunes with thousands of other spinifex flowers. Day in and day out, Spinnie and her family and friends would stay close to one another, holding onto each other to protect the sand dunes. Every day, they stood strong and still. There was nothing else to do. That was the life of a spinifex.

But Spinnie was different. She loved the ocean. She desired nothing more than to spin and roll and reach that water... oh, how wonderful it would be to get wet and let the waves gently rock you away.

"We must stay together, strong and still," her mother kept saying. "The winds are coming, and we must protect the dunes, we must protect our home."

But no matter how hard she tried, Spinnie couldn't stop thinking about the ocean. She imagined a world filled with fascinating creatures, vibrant colours, and endless discoveries...
"To the sea, to the sea, this is where I long to be," she would sing softly.

And then one day, just as they expected, the winds began to roar and the dunes trembled. Spinnie and her mother and all the other spinifex flowers braced themselves. Their bristly arms locked together, clinging to one another for support as the winds whipped around them. Together, they formed a strong barrier, protecting the fragile dunes, their precious home.

Days and weeks passed, and the winds finally softened to a gentle ocean breeze. All that was left in the air now was the beautiful scent of summer.

Spinnie knew this was her moment. She gathered all her strength and with a big, big push, she set free. She started rolling, spinning, twirling and playing with the breeze, saying hello to the crabs, the shells and the sea birds, and all the other creatures she met along the way.

The breeze gently led her to where she wanted to be – the water. The big, mighty ocean was right there, in front of her.

She looked behind, to the beach, one last time... then she took a deep breath and she dived in.

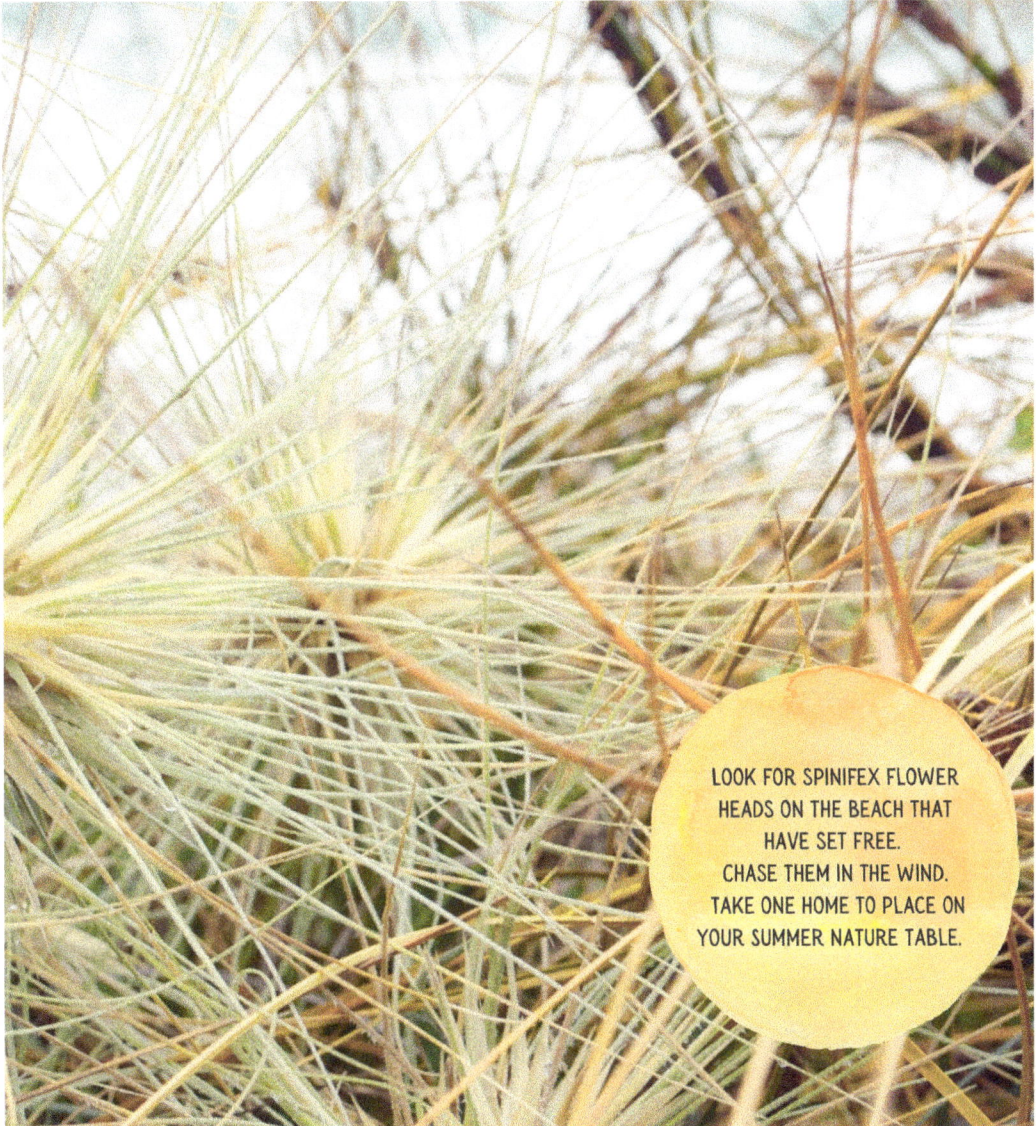

LOOK FOR SPINIFEX FLOWER HEADS ON THE BEACH THAT HAVE SET FREE.
CHASE THEM IN THE WIND.
TAKE ONE HOME TO PLACE ON YOUR SUMMER NATURE TABLE.

FEBRUARY

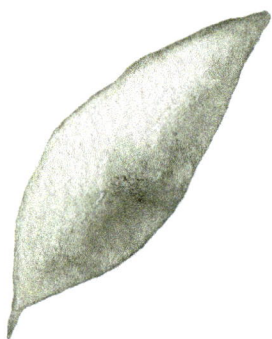

OPENING UP TO MOTHER EARTH'S BOUNTY

As February unfolds, and the warmth of summer starts to recede, the natural world stirs with new life and vitality. The north-easterly winds blow, bringing with them the gentle crash of waves and washing up bluebottles on our sandy shores. Snakes are basking in the sun, their scales glistening as they soak up the warmth in patches of grass or by the water's edge. The coast is hot and humid, mosquitos buzzing and breeding in the warm air.

We awaken to the magic of nature with a symphony of sounds. Bees, honeyeaters, rainbow lorikeets and rosellas loudly feast on flowering gums, banksias and grevilleas with such intense delight. Frogs and crickets are serenading their mates, singing love songs in the balmy summer dusks. Crick-crick, crick-crick, crick-crick... Quark-quark-quark...

There is, however, a hint of change in the air. Let's find ways to slow down and let the magic of summer linger for a moment longer. Celebrate the end of this season around a campfire with stories and songs, or try our delicious damper-on-a-stick recipe.

Fill your home with the sweet scent of basil as we explore the goodness of this sun-loving herb. We will be grinding, pounding, and making medicine to offer it to the full moon to invite abundance and prosperity into our lives.

EARTH MAGIC

BASIL

Basking in the sun, delicate white flowers are kissed by the bees, tender green leaves fill the air with their sweet fragrance. This month, we embark on an exploration of basil — a plant that invites us on a journey of connection, learning, and spiritual growth.

While we often associate basil with its culinary uses, there is so much more that this plant has to offer. As we'll discover, basil has a sacred and noble essence that has been revered since ancient times.

Let's start with its name. The word basil finds its roots in the ancient Greek term "basilikon" meaning 'royal'. This reflects the esteemed status that this herb has held throughout history due to its remarkable properties and contributions to well-being.

How many varieties of basil do you know? Surprisingly, there are over 60 known species of basil, with additional hybrids resulting from cross-pollination.

In this guide, we will focus our attention on two specific varieties: Sweet basil (*Ocimum basilicum*) and Tulsi, also known as holy basil (*Ocimum sanctum*). We will explore the characteristics, uses, and healing qualities of this plant, cultivating a deeper understanding of the immense wisdom it holds.

SWEET BASIL

Sweet basil, with its delightful aroma and vibrant green leaves, is a staple in our kitchens. Its earthy sweetness adds a tantalising flavour to our meals, making it a beloved herb in many culinary traditions. In Italy, my home country, basil is often paired with ripe, fresh tomatoes and sauces, and a few torn leaves are the essential finishing touch for a good pizza. Simply delicious!

Yet, the appeal of basil extends far beyond its culinary contributions. This herb is a true powerhouse of vitamins, minerals, and antioxidants, offering a range of health benefits. It plays a significant role in maintaining and promoting the long-term health of our respiratory tract, making it particularly valuable for those seeking respiratory support.

Drinking basil tea can settle stomach disorders and aid digestion, enhance mental clarity and focus, and it can help improve the quality of our sleep. The vibrant green colour of basil is often associated with the heart chakra, making it a herb that promotes not only physical well-being but also emotional healing and balance.

In addition to its medicinal properties, basil serves as a natural repellent for bugs and insects. Pluck a couple of leaves and rub them on the skin to alleviate itchiness from insect bites or follow the recipe to make our super easy bugs-away repellent spray.

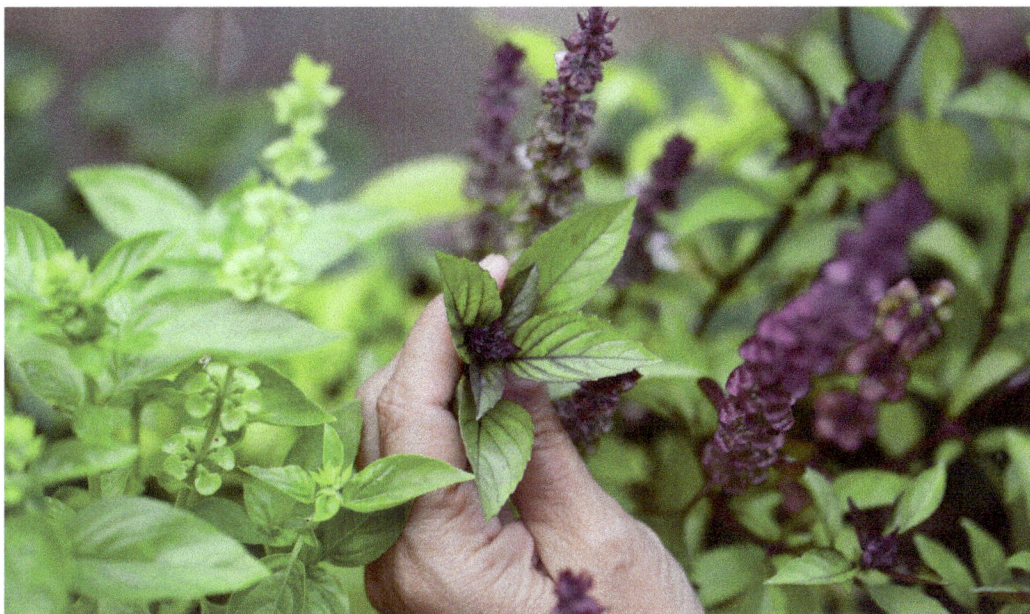

TULSI (HOLY BASIL)

Tulsi, also known as holy basil, possesses a rich history deeply rooted in spiritual and medicinal practices. Revered as a sacred herb in Indian culture for centuries, tulsi is renowned for its calming properties and its ability to promote overall well-being, harmony, and spiritual growth.

Tulsi can be recognised by its long bare stems and slightly hairy leaves, which can vary in colour from green to purple. The plant produces long spikes of flowers and has a pungent aroma with a peppery spiciness.

Largely used in Ayurvedic and traditional Chinese medicine, tulsi is known as the Queen of herbs. From its leaves to its seeds, it is considered a tonic for the body, mind, and spirit. Whether consumed, burned, or enjoyed as a herbal tea, this humble plant offers numerous health benefits. Let's explore some.

Helps you stay calm and focused
Tulsi has a calming effect on the brain. If you're feeling stressed, anxious, or struggling with concentration and memory, tulsi can lend a helping hand. By steeping a few leaves in hot water and sipping the herbal tea, you may notice an uplifting effect on your mood and mental clarity.

Natural mosquito repellent
Tulsi serves as an effective insect repellent, keeping insects and mosquitoes at bay. Place a few stems in water within your home or rub a few leaves on your body and your child's skin. It's perfect for this time of year.

Natural air purifier
With its refreshing and calming scent, tulsi fills your home with a sweet fragrance that promotes a positive mood. It also absorbs harmful gases present in the air, contributing to a clean and fresh environment.

Fights infections and boosts the immune system
Tulsi is rightly called the 'Mother medicine of nature' and 'Queen of herbs' due to its remarkable ability to assist the body in fighting against colds, coughs, and other infections. It possesses anti-inflammatory, antibacterial, antifungal, and antiviral properties. Its leaves are rich in fat-soluble vitamins A and K, as well as vitamin C. Additionally, they serve as an excellent source of minerals such as calcium, phosphorus, iron, zinc, and magnesium.

Benefits the skin
Tulsi aids in the elimination of blemishes and acne, making it beneficial for adults. Due to its antioxidant content, it also helps prevent premature ageing. Incorporating tulsi into bathing water or simply washing your child's face with it can help safeguard against various skin infections.

Tulsi is generally considered safe for children and is widely used in Ayurvedic medicine. However, if you have any doubts or concerns, it is always best to consult with your paediatrician, naturopath, or family doctor.

TULSI CAN GROW QUITE BIG AND SPREAD QUICKLY, SO IF YOU HAVE LIMITED SPACE IN YOUR GARDEN, IT IS BEST TO KEEP IT IN A BEAUTIFUL POT.

INVITING A GODDESS INTO YOUR HOME

In India, tulsi holds a sacred place as it is believed to embody the earthly presence of Lakshmi, the Hindu goddess of abundance, prosperity, beauty, grace, and generosity. According to Hindu traditions, on full moon nights the goddess Lakshmi visits each home, showering its inhabitants with blessings of wealth and prosperity.

Just like the goddess herself, tulsi carries blessings and positive energy into the home. That is why it is a common practice in India to keep a tulsi plant outside the house, near the front door. Tulsi also grows abundantly around temples, symbolising its significance in invoking blessings.

By inviting tulsi into your home or garden, you can create an atmosphere infused with positive vibes and attract abundance and prosperity. The presence of this sacred plant serves as a reminder of the divine grace and blessings that flow into our lives.

BUGS-AWAY INSECT REPELLENT

Let's begin with a quick science lesson on insect repellents. Repellents work by interfering with the sensory systems of insects, making it difficult for them to detect their targets (aka, you!) and prompting them to go away. There are several natural volatile compounds that can be used as repellents. Some of these include pyrethrins, terpinen-4-ol, methyl-nonyl-ketone, geraniol, estragole, citronella, limonene, and nerolidol.

Plants like citronella, geranium, and melaleuca, which are commonly known for their insect repellent properties, produce at least one of these substances. However, basil stands out as it contains not just one, but four of these compounds, making it highly effective in keeping those pesky insects at bay. Let's use it to make our own natural bug spray to use during our outdoors adventures.

Things to gather:

- fresh basil leaves (sweet basil or tulsi)
- filtered water
- witch hazel
- a spray bottle

Directions. Cut a few sprigs of basil and separate the leaves from the stems. You will need about 1 cup of leaves. Children can help by chopping the basil into smaller pieces using child-safe scissors or their hands.
Place the freshly picked leaves in a heatproof jar and cover them completely with 1/2 a cup of boiling water. Close the jar and let it sit for 4 hours.
Strain the liquid into a spray bottle, making sure to squeeze out any remaining liquid from the leaves using a masher or fork.
Add 1/2 a cup of witch hazel to the spray bottle. If desired, you can also add 10 drops of basil or lemon eucalyptus essential oil for added potency.
Gently shake the bottle to mix the ingredients together. Apply directly on any exposed skin to protect against mosquito and other bug bites.

Note

Another simple way to use basil as a mosquito repellent is to rub a few leaves directly on exposed skin or keep a basil plant on your windowsill. You can also place a few stems on your dining table when eating outdoors or make smudge sticks to burn in your home.

Please be aware of the following risks:

Avoid using holy basil if you are allergic or sensitive to it or other plants from the mint family (Lamiaceae). Use caution if you are pregnant or trying to conceive, or if you take anticoagulant (blood-thinning) medication.

FULL MOON

SMUDGE STICKS

Smudging is the practice of slowly burning bundles of herbs and flowers – called smudge sticks – to cleanse and bless people and places. It's a lovely way to freshen up a space, clear away negative energy and bring in positive vibes.

To create your own smudge sticks for attracting prosperity, abundance, and blessings, start with fresh or dried tulsi and add a combination of herbs from the list provided below.

Lavender: Lavender cleanses, protects, and brings happiness, healing, and calmness to the home.

White sage: This is the most commonly used herb for smudging. Often associated with purification and cleansing rituals, white sage is said to brings wisdom, clarity and protection.

Rosemary: A powerful cleanser for your home and aura, rosemary is known for bringing energy and clarity.

Rose: With its connection to the heart, burning rose promotes love, healing, and self-care.

Eucalyptus: Smudging with eucalyptus brings a sense of balance, clarity, and emotional well-being. It can also awaken your spirit and encourage deeper connections.

Directions. Start by gathering your ingredients and arrange them on a table. Place the largest leaves or stems at the same level as one another.

Cut a long piece of twine. Tie a simple loose knot on one end of the string, and then tighten it around the stems to bind the bundle together. Using the long end of the string, begin wrapping it tightly around the bundle, spiralling up towards the top. As you wrap, fold in any stray sprigs and tuck them under the string to keep everything secure.

Once you reach the top, keep wrapping crisscrossing the twine as you head back down toward the base. Tie the loose end to the original knot at the base of the stick.

If you wish, you can add decorative flowers or a small crystal.

If using fresh plants, hang your smudge sticks upside down in a sunny spot and allow the herbs to dry completely before using.

When smudging, light one end of your bundle with a match. Blow out the flame, and let the bundle continue to burn, positioning into a shell, glass or clay bowl. After you smudge, throw open the windows to help get rid of any negative energy.

Remember to approach smudging with respect and mindfulness, allowing the smoke to carry your intentions and blessings.

FULL MOONS INVITE US INTO A SPACE OF STILLNESS AND INTROSPECTION. IT'S A TIME FOR DREAMING, REACHING FOR THE STARS, AND SURRENDERING TO THE NATURAL RHYTHMS OF THE UNIVERSE.

IN THE KITCHEN

MAKE TRADITIONAL PESTO

Born in Liguria, a beautiful region situated in northern Italy, pesto is an uncooked cold sauce made with basil. Its vibrant green colour and delicious taste is loved by both children and adults and can be a wonderful addition to many dishes.

Making pesto at home is not only fun but also easy. This is the traditional recipe of pesto Genovese, in which the ingredients are "pestati", which means ground by hand using a marble mortar and pestle – if you have one at home, it's a great opportunity to try it out!

Note. A marble mortar and pestle is the best tool to make pesto because it allows the basil to retain its vibrant colour. The heat generated by food processors tends to oxidise the plant, resulting in a darker and slightly bitter sauce. There is a trick, however... keep reading to find out!

Ingredients:

- 50g of fresh basil leaves (about 60-65 leaves)
- 1/2 cup of extra virgin olive oil
- 70g parmigiano reggiano, grated
- 30g pecorino, grated
- 2 peeled garlic cloves (1 clove for every 30 basil leaves)
- 1 tbsp of pine nuts
- 4 or 5 grains of coarse salt
- grana padano, grated

Method. Wash the basil leaves in cold water, then place them in a bowl with ice for a couple of minutes. If using a food processor, chill the blades and bowl in the fridge for about 10 minutes. This step helps maintain a sweet and bright green pesto.

Pat dry all the basil leaves carefully with a paper towel.

Mortar and pestle method
Start by crushing the garlic cloves in the mortar with the coarse salt until it becomes creamy. Add the pine nuts and continue grinding to combine. Gradually add the basil leaves, a few at a time, while grinding with a gentle, circular movement.

Once all the ingredients are well combined, add the grated cheeses and then the extra virgin olive oil, slowly incorporating them into the mixture. Your basil pesto is ready!

Food processor method
Place the chilled basil leaves, pine nuts, and grated cheeses in the food processor. Pulse briefly to chop the ingredients coarsely. Add the coarse salt and pulse again. Slowly pour the olive oil into the mixture while blending at low speed, scraping down the sides as needed. Continue blending until all the ingredients come together, creating a creamy, delicious sauce.

Refrigerate the pesto and use within three days, or freeze it into ice cubes for future use. Enjoy your homemade pesto on pasta, spread on sandwiches, or drizzled on fresh tomatoes.

Notes. If using on pasta, remember to reserve 1-2 tablespoons of the cooking water to mix through the pesto – it will create a smoother consistency.

Always cover leftover pesto with a thin layer of extra virgin olive oil to keep it fresh.

Substitutions. For a vegan version, substitute the cheese with 3-4 tablespoons of nutritional yeast. Replace pine nuts with walnuts or sunflower seeds for a nut-free option.

NATURE PLAY

MORTAR AND PESTLE SENSORY PLAY

If your children have been watching you – or even better, helping – make basil pesto, they will likely be delighted at the chance of using a mortar and pestle in their play. This versatile tool is perfect for children as young as two years old, as it helps build focus, concentration, fine motor skills, hand strength, and allows them to tap into their imaginative side.

The simple, ancient act of grinding herbs and spices is centering, gratifying, and children love experimenting with different scent combinations, colours, and textures to create magic potions, brew fairy teas, make natural paint, and inks. Grinding flowers and herbs releases their aroma and essential oils, engaging our senses.

Guide your children by demonstrating how to safely hold the pestle. If they start banging, gently remind them that tools need to be treated with care.

SENSORY PLAY INVITATIONS

Here are some ideas to explore with your child using a mortar and pestle.

Make green paint
Encourage your child to grind basil leaves in the mortar and pestle and see if they can extract some colour. Mix the ground leaves with a little water and explore painting with the homemade green paint.

Create your own perfume
Grind basil leaves and mix them with water to create a fragrant concoction. Pour it into a spray bottle and let your child spray it on plants, flowers, teddy bears, or even themselves.

Green playdough

Grind basil leaves (and add a touch of spirulina or matcha powder for extra green colour) with a little water. Mix with flour, salt, oil and cream of tartar to make your own green playdough.

Explore pounding and grinding

Encourage your child to experiment with other materials like flower petals to make potpourri, seeds and nuts to add to their muesli, or eggshells for the compost.
You can also make chalk paint by grinding pieces of chalk and mixing it with water. Perfect to create colourful designs on the driveway or sidewalk!

These are just a few ideas to spark your child's imagination and creativity. Have fun and see what other creative possibilities you and your child can discover together!

GRIND FLOWER PETALS AND HERBS TO MIX WITH PLAYDOUGH.

CELEBRATE THE END OF SUMMER AROUND CAMPFIRE

Summer is coming to an end and it's the perfect excuse to gather friends and family around a cosy campfire! Our end of summer celebrations always include cooking *damper on a stick*. We enjoy it with raw honey and a sprinkle of cinnamon, but you can try savoury toppings like homemade pesto, too.

Children love finding the perfect cooking stick, which adds an element of fun and adventure to the experience.

EASY CAMPFIRE DAMPER BREAD

Ingredients:

- 2 cups (300g) self-raising flour
- 200ml warm water
- 2 tbsp (30ml) olive oil
- 1 tsp salt
- 1 tsp sugar

Method. In a large bowl, mix all the ingredients with a wooden spoon. No kneading required. Cover the bowl and let the dough rise in a warm place for about one hour, until it doubles in size. With floured hands, shape the dough into a ball and divide it into 8 pieces on a floured surface.

Meanwhile...

Ask your children to find the perfect cooking stick! It should be green, as long as their arm, and as thick as their thumb. Once they find it, give it a little clean and scrape off the bark from the tip. Older children can practise whittling with a kid-friendly pocket knife (check our website for recommendations).

Shaping the dough

Stretch the dough with your hands and roll it into a long sausage shape. Starting from the point, twist it around the stick. Gently squeeze the dough with your palm to remove any gaps and secure it to the stick. This step is important to prevent the damper from opening and falling into the flames while cooking.

Cooking over a campfire

Hold or prop up your stick over the fire, making sure it's positioned over hot embers - keep rotating the stick until all sides of the damper are cooked and turn golden.

Use a napkin or paper towel to slide the bread off the stick. Careful, as it will be hot! Fill the damper with your favourite toppings and enjoy.

Empower children with knowledge about fire
and the wisdom to handle it responsibly.

MARCH

PLANTING SEEDS OF KINDNESS

Riberry trees (lilly pilly) are heavy with juicy berries. The fruits of geebungs (Persoonia) are soft and ripe. The weather is unpredictable, and winds begin to shift, just as one of our most beloved native trees – the *Melaleuca quinquenervia*, or broad-leaved paperbark tree - begins to bloom. An explosion of white and creamy blossoms fills the air with their sweet scent, inviting birds, bats and bees to an abundant feast.

Light and dark find their balance, as we approach the equinox. The long days of summer are winding down and we transition into autumn, the season of the Earth element. The Earth symbolises stability and groundedness – our roots. Within us, Earth is family and friends. It is the fabric of life, the bonds of love and community that hold us together.

Autumn is harvest time, but just as importantly, it is a time when seeds are collected and protected from the colder months ahead. With our love and care, they will grow and bloom in next year's garden. A perfect balance of giving and receiving.

In the garden of our mind, we plant tender seeds of kindness and gratitude.

EARTH MAGIC

BROAD-LEAVED PAPERBARK TREE

Thank you, paperbark tree, for your layers of practical and healing gifts. For your medicine, and your protection. Thank you for the sweet nectar you provide to our bird friends after their long, tiring journey. Thank you for your curly, twirly wrinkly branches – strong under our feet but gentle on our knees. Up there – our head immersed in clouds of white, honey-scented flowers – we feel free, strong, and wise, just like you.

A native tree to Australia, the *Melaleuca quinquenervia* is commonly known as broad-leaved tea tree or paperbark tree. One of this tree's most remarkable characteristics is the multiple layers of thin, paper-like bark that envelop the trunk, providing protection and aiding its survival during fire season. Often confused with the *Melaleuca alternifolia*, the species from which tea tree oil is derived, the broad-leaved paperbark can be identified by the presence of five veins on the leaf blade, derived from the Latin words "quinque" meaning 'five', and "nervus" meaning 'veins' or 'nerves'.

The Melaleuca tree holds significant cultural importance and was utilised in many traditional practices. Aboriginal Australians used its bark to create waterproof roofing for their shelters, or soaked it in water to wrap and cook food such as fish, emu, or kangaroo over an open fire. Babies were born onto the softest sheets of paperbark, which would keep them dry and warm.

From the grey-green leaves of the *Melaleuca quinquenervia*, we extract a medicinal oil known as niaouli. Niaouli oil possesses similar antiseptic and cleansing properties as tea tree oil, albeit with a gentler and sweeter aroma, evoking the fresh and earthy scents of the Australian bush. Niaouli oil is frequently employed in treating colds and coughs, and it is renowned for its calming and refreshing qualities, as well as its immune-boosting benefits.

DID YOU KNOW?

The soft inner bark of Melaleuca trees is known as a bush band-aid. Covered by a white powder of antiseptic magic, it can be safely applied to small wounds and insect bites while you are out and about exploring.

THE LEGEND OF EELEMANI

A tale from the Bundjalung people of the Ballina region in Northern New South Wales.

"This is the legend of Eelemani, a beautiful princess who must leave her true love and travel through the bushland of coastal New South Wales.

The journey was long and the wild trail was unknown to Eelemani. She was concerned that the return to her loved one and family would be difficult. Eelemani was no ordinary princess and so she spoke to the gods of the Earth and planets and was rewarded with special seeds that were to be sown along the trails.

As Eelemani walked through the forests, the bell birds called reassuringly and willie wagtails followed protectively through their territory. The special seeds were scattered on the moist, fertile forest soil. Falling to the ground, they grew roots and shoots and flew towards the sunlight. So remarkable were these trees that their beautiful white paper bark stood out from all the other trees. At night the polished sheen reflected the light of the Moon showing the trail.

Eelemani felt so safe knowing that the gods had given her such a powerful marker to protect her on her journey. And so the trees of Eelemani flourished and over the aeons of time the Bundjalung people came to learn of their magical properties. Just as the trees had protected Eelemani, the leaves were found to protect them against infection and skin ailments."[1]

EASY BREATHE STEAM

Make this easy steam to relieve coughing, nasal congestion and headaches.

Things to gather:

- leaves from a Melaleuca tree
- water

Directions. Crush the leaves gently with your hands and add to a pot full of water. Place the pot on the stove and heat the water until it comes to a boil. Turn off the heat and let the leaves steep for another 10-15 minutes. Keep the decoction on your kitchen bench or on your bedside table and breathe in deeply, giving thanks to the tree for the healing provided.

Alternatively, you can crush the leaves into a bowl of hot water, place a towel over your head, and inhale deeply through your nose.

Please supervise and assist children during this process to prevent burns.

FULL MOON

SAND PAINTING

Sand painting is an ancient art form practised by various cultures, including Indigenous Australian communities and Native American tribes. Intricate sand paintings were created to exist only a few hours – exposed to the elements, they would be allowed to gradually fade and return to the Earth.

In this craft, we will use naturally coloured sand and glue to create a painting of the beautiful full moon that illuminates our night skies before the autumn equinox.

While you create, take a moment to feel the texture of the sand. Allow yourself to be inspired by the delicate layers of the paperbark tree. Did you notice that this tree likes to grow on coastal dunes and sandy plains?

Things to gather:

- fine sand
- natural paint (make your own using the recipe in Nature Play)
- glue
- glass jars
- shakers with perforated tops

Directions. Start by placing the sand in a glass jar and adding the desired amount of paint. Shake the jar vigorously to coat the sand with the colourful pigments. Have your child trace the shape of the Moon on a large piece of paper. Cover the paper with glue and quickly sprinkle the coloured sand onto it.

Wait until completely dry, then blow any excess sand off.

IN THE KITCHEN

COOKING WITH PAPERBARK

Paperbark adds a lovely earthy, smoky flavour to fish, poultry, and vegetables. Wash the bark before using it, then soak it in water to soften.

LEMON INFUSED FISH WITH HERB BUTTER

This is one of my favourite recipes for cooking with paperbark, adapted from a recipe by chef Mark Olive.

Ingredients:

- 30g organic butter, at room temperature
- salt flakes
- 2 tbsp ground lemon myrtle
- 2 lemons, 1 juiced, 1 cut into 8 slices
- 1/2 a cup macadamia oil
- fish of choice, whole
- large sheets of paperbark

Method. Preheat the oven to 180°C . If cooking over a campfire, wait until you have embers for slow, steady-cooking.
Start by making the herb butter: combine butter, salt flakes and 1 tsp of lemon myrtle. Stir in lemon juice, spoon onto a sheet of plastic wrap and roll up tightly to form a log. Refrigerate for 30 min to firm.

Meanwhile, combine macadamia oil with 3 tsp lemon myrtle. Rub over fish and brush paperbark with what's remaining. Place fish and lemon slices on the paperbark sheets, roll up, gather ends and tie with cooking twine to form a parcel. Place on an oven tray, sprinkle with water, cover tray with foil and roast for 20 minutes or until the fish is just cooked. Serve with herb butter.

NATURE PLAY

PAPERBARK NATURE JOURNAL

This charming little book can be used as a nature journal, sketch pad, or as a photo album. Paperbark is easy to handle and very versatile, and will give your creations a beautiful natural look. Can you find other ways to use it?

Things to gather:

- a piece of paperbark
- sheets of recycled or watercolour paper
- a hole punch
- a thin stick

- scissors
- string
- watercolours, earth paint, dry flowers and leaves (optional)

Directions. Begin with the paperbark. Cut it into a long rectangular shape, ensuring that it's thick enough but still foldable. Place it between heavy books for a few hours to flatten. This will become the cover of your journal.

Cut the paper to approximately the same size as your cover. Place a stack of paper inside the paperbark cover, and fold it in the middle. Punch two holes through the paper and cover.

Cut or break your stick to about the same height as your book. Thread through the holes and secure with string.

Now you can decorate and personalise your journal – use watercolours or earth pigments, glue your favourite leaves on it or wrap it with beautiful twine.

MAKING NATURAL PAINT

During one of our nature play gatherings, I had the pleasure of meeting Phil, a talented artist and a wonderful human being. He was there with his three year old grandson, and we instantly connected, chatting about art and nature. On that day, Phil introduced me to the fascinating world of natural pigments.

As we crushed ochre to create body paint for a camouflage game, he showed me how we can make paint and inks not only from rocks and minerals but also from plants, flowers, nuts, seeds, soil, and even coffee grounds! I was captivated. Since then, I've been experimenting with creating inks, dyes, and various types of paint using natural materials.

While there is always some trial and error involved, I enjoy the process tremendously. The children love joining me in making these paints, and the best part is that once we're finished, we can return everything back to the Earth without causing any harm. It's a sustainable and eco-friendly way to explore our creativity and connect with nature.

Getting started

There are so many ways to create natural paints using powdered herbal pigments, which can be easily found at your local bulk food shop. These paints can add beautiful colours to your artwork.

Here are some examples of pigments you can use:

- Green spirulina for green
- Ground turmeric for yellow
- Paprika for light orange
- Pink pitaya and beetroot powder for pink/purple
- Blue spirulina and butterfly pea powder for blue
- Ground cinnamon and coffee grounds for brown

I personally keep small jars of these pigments with all my art supplies. They are a wonderful addition to any creative project!

Things to gather:

your chosen natural pigment from the list above or other sources
gum arabic (available at art supply stores)
honey
clove oil or whole cloves (optional)
clean jars with lids

Prepare the paint mix. In a clean jar, mix the pigment and gum arabic in a ratio of 1 part gum to 4 parts pigment. Stir well until the mixture is thoroughly blended. You can make larger batches of the paint mix and store them in a dry place with the lid on for extended use.

Make the paint. Take a small bowl or jar and combine a teaspoon of the powdered paint mix with water and a drop of honey. Start with a small amount of water and gradually add more to achieve the desired consistency. Mix the ingredients well until they are fully blended. Your watercolour paint is now ready to use!

Use paint sparingly and only pour what you need. Any leftover paint can be transferred to a mason jar, with the addition of a whole clove if desired, and stored in the refrigerator for future use.

EARTH PIGMENTS

While beautiful natural colours can be achieved with fresh or dried plant material, there is something quite special about creating with Earth pigments. Earth pigments are a gift from the Earth – natural pigments made from soil, minerals, and clay that have been ground into a fine powder.

Next time you head out for a walk in the bush or on the beach, keep an eye out for ochre and rocks with vibrant colours. You'll be amazed at the range of deep browns, orange tones, warm reds, lighter yellows and creams that you can find.

To test if a rock can be used as a pigment, wet it and try writing with it on another rock. Children find this process so fascinating! If it does, you can grind the rock into a fine powder using a mortar and pestle or by crushing it with a larger stone on a hard surface. Transfer the powder into a seashell or small lid, and mix it with a few drops of water. You can use it as watercolour or make body paint.

Remember
Please forage responsibly. Before you take anything with you, make a deep connection with the Earth and ask for permission. Take small amounts only.

OCHRE IS OF THE EARTH

In Australia, ochre has been used for thousands of years by Aboriginal and Torres Strait Islander people to tell stories through art and to practise ceremony. Mixed with animal fat, it was rubbed into wooden tools and ceremonial items to preserve the wood and prolong its use.

Ochre is also widely used as medicine. When ingested, some ochres have an antacid effect on the digestive system. Red ochre, due to its rich mineral content, is often used to protect the skin from the elements of weather, insect bites, ticks and fleas and is also excellent in caring for wounds.

Ochre is a precious resource. It lives in the Earth, and should always be used with reverence and respect.[2]

MINDFULNESS

SEEDS OF KINDNESS CARDS

Imagine if your child's painting could transform into beautiful flowers. That's the magic of this lovely craft! Using only natural materials, these cards can be planted directly in the soil, returning to Mother Earth and beginning a new life cycle.

Things to gather:

- recycled cardboard or watercolour paper
- natural paint
- natural glue
- flower seeds

Directions. Start by cutting the paper into heart shapes or any desired shape, and let your child paint them with the natural watercolour paint you made this month. While the paint is drying, prepare the natural glue using the recipe below.

Once the glue is ready, spread a thin layer onto each card and sprinkle flower seeds on top. We recommend using marigolds and cosmos, which you can collect from your own garden by harvesting the seeds from mature flower heads. You can also buy flower seeds from a garden nursery or check if your local library offers a seed swapping program.

Gift to someone special or plant in your garden. Watch as your acts of kindness grow into beautiful flowers, spreading joy and love wherever they bloom.

NATURAL GLUE

Things to gather:

- 1/2 cup flour
- 1/2 to 1 cup cold water

There are many recipes for homemade, natural glue – usually made by mixing flour or cornstarch with water. Do a bit of research and find the recipe that works for you. This is the one that I use, which is really easy to whip up in minutes.

Directions. In a saucepan, whisk together flour and cold water. Start with equal portions of flour and water, then gradually add more water as needed. Heat the mixture until it boils and thickens. Remove from heat and allow to cool before using.

Store in a sealed container.

APRIL

GROUNDING, CONNECTING WITH THE EARTH

Deciduous trees are changing colours – a blaze of red, amber, and gold. Soon their branches will be bare. Catch a falling leaf and make a wish.

Black bean pods are gathered and treasured by intrepid little hands – floating along creeks and water streams, they become tiny boats in search of big adventures. Sea mullets start their journey towards the open waters to spawn. Gannets arrive to hunt – watch them plunge-dive at incredible speed into the vastness of our oceans.

During this month, as we deepen our exploration of the Earth element, we ground ourselves in the tactile experience of clay. With our hands immersed in this precious gift from the Earth, we connect with its nurturing energy. The malleable clay becomes our medium for creation, allowing us to mould and shape our intentions.

EARTH MAGIC

CLAY

This month, we embark on a journey into the fascinating world of clay.
A natural sediment formed through the intricate processes of rock transformation, clay unveils a world of endless possibilities.

What makes clay truly remarkable is its malleable and tactile nature. Its soft and yielding texture responds to every touch, twist, and pull, offering so many opportunities for exploration and experimentation. As we engage with clay, our fingers sink into its cool and smooth surface, delighting in the sensory experience it provides. Its earthy scent grounds us, bringing a sense of comfort and connection to the natural world. Working and playing with clay becomes an invitation to awaken our senses.

CLAY IS A MATERIAL THAT SPEAKS OF THE HISTORY OF HUMANKIND

Hands – our primal and most unique tool – plunge into the clay, breaking it into small pieces, rolling, pinching, squishing, and sinking into the material with great pleasure. Children first learn to shape clay with their fists, palms, or fingertips, experimenting as they go with creating three-dimensional forms, discovering gravity, layering, pressure and balancing of volumes. With each interaction, they discover new textures, forms, and possibilities, fostering a new sense of wonder and discovery.

Clay is experienced through all its stages, from moist to dry. At the beginning it's silky, soft, squishy, and slippery. Then it becomes gritty, rough, and solid. Crushed, powdered, clay meets with water and comes back to life, regaining its plastic ability. This tactile engagement nourishes the senses and fuels curiosity, inspiring open-ended play and imaginative exploration.

With clay we connect to an important natural resource that has been used by human beings for thousands of years in the creation of art objects. Clay comes from the Earth, born from the very fabric of our planet. It can be reused and recycled, and at the end of its life cycle, it can be returned to the Earth. This reinforces the values of sustainability and responsible use of resources that we strive to instil in our children.

CLAY'S HEALING PROPERTIES

The healing properties of clay have been recognised and utilised across cultures for millennia. Rich in minerals, clay offers the benefits of detoxification and remineralisation for the body.

One of the most commonly used healing clays is bentonite, a type of clay of volcanic origin. Bentonite acts as a natural absorbent, effectively drawing out toxins, heavy metals, and chemicals from the body. At the same time, it replenishes us with essential minerals.

Clay's astringent properties make it a popular ingredient in skincare products. It can be applied topically to address various skin conditions, including bug bites or stings, cuts, eczema, psoriasis, minor burns, lymphedema, and inflammation. Its healing qualities help promote scar formation and stimulate the skin's rejuvenation process.

You can create a simple face mask by mixing clay with water to form a smooth paste and applying it to your skin for a deep pore cleanse. As a facial mask, clay assists in purifying the skin by eliminating impurities and revitalising its appearance, enhancing circulation.

For targeted treatment, such as insect bites, a small amount of clay mixed with water can be applied to the affected area and covered with a band-aid.

Once again, Mother Nature has gifted us with a potent natural medicine!

DID YOU KNOW THAT YOU CAN FIND CLAY IN ITS RAW, NATURAL STATE QUITE EASILY IN NATURE? SOME GOOD PLACES TO SEARCH FOR YOUR OWN LOCAL CLAY ARE RIVERBANKS, OCEAN SHORES, OR CONSTRUCTION SITES.

FULL MOON

MOON PHASE GARLAND

Learn about the different phases of the Moon with this lovely clay garland.

Things to gather:

- air-dry clay
- baking paper
- a rolling pin
- a jar lid or round cookie cutter
- cotton twine
- a skewer or a stick for poking holes
- metallic paint (optional)
- dried flowers (optional)

Directions. Place the clay between two sheets of baking paper. Use a rolling pin to roll it out until you achieve a smooth, flat surface that is approximately 1/4" to 1/3" thick.

With a round cutter or lid, create seven circular shapes. Set one aside as your full moon.

Cut into each of the other rounds, stopping at 1/4, 1/2, and 3/4 of the way through to create the Moon waxing and waning effect. Flip one shape from each pair to make them mirror opposites.

Now take a skewer or stick and create holes at the top and bottom of each moon shape. Make sure to align the holes so that the moons will hang straight.

Allow the clay to dry completely, which may take approximately 24 to 48 hours. Cut a length of twine and thread it through the holes of the moons. To prevent them from sliding, tie a knot on the back of each shape and behind the last hole.

Finally, create a loop at the top end of the twine to hang your mobile. Now you have a charming moon garland ready to adorn your space!

Optional. You can paint the moons with metallic paint to add a touch of shine and enhance their appearance. You can also add dried flowers to the garland by attaching them to the twine between the moon shapes

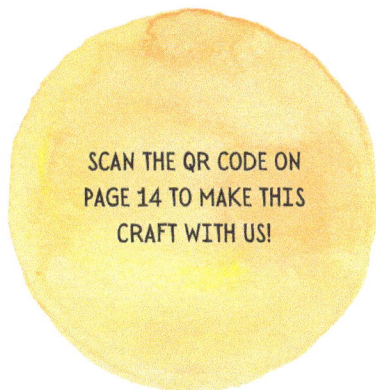

SCAN THE QR CODE ON
PAGE 14 TO MAKE THIS
CRAFT WITH US!

IN THE KITCHEN

APPLES

As the season transitions into autumn, one of the delights we anticipate is the arrival of fresh, juicy apples!
Crisp and deliciously sweet, but low on the glycemic index, apples are cooling and refreshing when eaten raw, and soft and soothing when cooked (as well as a great constipation relief for babies and children).

Apples lend themselves beautifully to cooking and baking – the aroma of baked apples brings a sense of comfort and cosiness to our homes. Such an autumn treat!

Here below are two of my favourite *forest snacks* - yummy treats we enjoy while we are out exploring in nature.

APPLE AND NUT BUTTER RINGS

A healthy and delicious snack that takes one minute to prepare.

Ingredients:

- an apple
- favourite nut butter

Method. Slice an apple crosswise into thin rings. Your little assistant chef can now spread creamy nut butter onto each ring. Sprinkle with granola, chia seeds, coconut shreds or any other favourite topping (optional). Enjoy!

APPLE CINNAMON CUPS

When the crisp autumn mornings arrive, there's nothing quite like cosying up with a blanket, enjoying these delightful apple cinnamon cups with your loved ones. This activity is so fun and delicious, and of course the best part is that once you finish drinking, you get to eat your cup!

Ingredients:

- fresh, juicy apples
- cinnamon sticks
- apple juice or apple cider

Method. Begin by carefully cutting off the tops of the apples, creating a small opening. With a spoon, gently scoop out the flesh from inside the apples, making sure to remove the core. (Don't let the apple's insides go to waste – they can be saved and used in delicious apple cinnamon muffins or other tasty recipes).

Pour apple juice or cider in your hollowed-out apples. Insert a cinnamon stick into each apple cup – it will infuse the drink with its warm, delightful flavour, and double up as a straw.

SHAKE THE APPLE TREE

This modified version of the classic nursery rhyme is a favourite autumn circle time song at our nature play gatherings. Children can accompany the words with actions – shaking, blowing, stirring, shivering from cold.

> Shake, shake the apple tree. Apples red and rosy
>
> Shake, shake the apple tree. Apples red and rosy
>
> One for you, one for me
>
> Shake, shake the apple tree
>
> Blow, blow the leaves away. Windy windy weather
>
> Blow, blow the leaves away. Windy windy weather
>
> Blow them here, blow them there
>
> Blow, blow the leaves away
>
> Stir, stir the pumpkin soup. Stir it with a wooden spoon
>
> Stir, stir the pumpkin soup. Stir it with a wooden spoon
>
> Goodbye summer, bright and gold
>
> Welcome autumn, red and cold

NATURE PLAY

WORKING WITH CLAY

Most children, when presented with a piece of soft clay, are instinctively motivated to explore its inviting, soft, and responsive sensory qualities. They might poke it, squeeze it, hit it, pick it up, and pound it down. Soon they realise it can be shaped. Each time they interact with the clay, the clay adjusts and responds.

While these transformations may seem insignificant to adults, they hold a sense of magic and wonder for young children. As the clay takes shape, a world of possibilities unfolds before them... What happens if I try this? What else can I create? What is the next step to achieve what I am envisioning?

As always, we want to allow children the time and space to experiment at their own pace. There are, however, a few things adults can do to support and facilitate their exploration.

CHOOSING THE RIGHT TYPE OF CLAY

If you don't have access to a kiln or a potter who can fire your creations, it's best to opt for air-dry clay, which is readily available in white or terracotta varieties.

White clay, with its smaller particles, offers a softer and smoother texture, making it suitable for children and beginners. Terracotta clay is more robust and better suited for sculpting larger objects or working with slabs.

When setting up a play invitation for your child, ensure that the clay is soft and easy to work with. If it feels too firm, you can add moisture and knead it (wedging) until it reaches a pliable state. This will make the clay more manageable and enjoyable to create with.

PREPARING THE WORK ENVIRONMENT

To prevent the clay from sticking, it's best to use a hessian-covered table or board. If hessian is not available, you can use a ceramic tile or even a chopping board covered with a large sheet of baking paper.

Let children fully explore the clay with their hands first. Once they have grasped the basic techniques of manipulating clay, natural materials such as shells and sticks can be used for mark-making and creating texture. Wooden clay tools can also be added at a later stage. Provide small sponges for smoothing, and a small bowl of water for dampening and washing hands.

GETTING READY TO EXPLORE

To start, offer each child a grapefruit-sized amount of clay, divided into two or three pieces. Offer more only when needed or requested. For younger children, starting with smaller amounts of clay can feel less overwhelming and more manageable, fostering a sense of confidence and curiosity. **Resist the temptation of offering too much** – this humble beginning can lead to endless possibilities of exploration and innovation.

Avoid flattening the clay into a pancake shape – instead model different techniques and demonstrate basic movements such as pinching, poking, rolling, tearing and piling.

If working with more experienced children, you can introduce additional techniques to expand their clay skills. These may include coiling, making pinch pots, shaping, and securely joining parts with slip to construct more complex objects. It's important to guide children in joining pieces firmly and remind them to avoid rolling the clay too thin, as this can lead to crumbling and breakage once it dries.

Offer clay regularly. One-off experiences do not provide the opportunity to extend their skills, deepen their understanding, or experiment with new ideas.

CARING FOR THE CLAY

Clay needs to be kept moist to remain workable. After each use, cover the clay with a damp cloth and store it in a plastic bag within an airtight container. If the clay becomes hard, it means that the moisture has evaporated and it needs to be rehydrated. Encourage children to participate in caring for the clay:

- After use, roll the clay into small-sized balls and create a thumb hole in each ball, filling it with water. Store these clay balls in an airtight container in a cool place to keep them moist and pliable.
- Collect pieces of unused, dried up clay and break them into smaller fragments using a hammer or roller. Soak the fragments in water and allow them to soften for at least 1-2 hours. Drain off any excess water and place the softened clay on a cloth on top of newspaper to dry to a manageable consistency before using it again. Children love breaking up and re-wetting dry clay, let this be their job!

THE ROLE OF ADULTS

Our attitude towards clay and other types of 'messy play' has a significant impact on how our children perceive and engage with it. Show a positive attitude and embrace the messiness of the medium. By demonstrating your own enjoyment and willingness to get your hands dirty, you encourage children to do the same without fear or hesitation.

Here are some key ways in which we can enhance the clay experience for our children (and ourselves!).

Use rich language. Discuss elements like form, texture and colour, but also don't be afraid to introduce specific technical terms, such as coiling, modelling, sculpting, decorating, slip, glaze, and firing.

As children explore the wonderful world of clay, it's important to create a **safe and encouraging environment** where they feel free to express themselves. Avoid asking "What is it?" as this limits their creativity and may make them feel pressured to conform to specific shapes or forms. Instead observe, acknowledge their progress, and ask open-ended questions that encourage them to share their thoughts and ideas.

Offer assistance. Clay work takes practice and patience and we are presented with ample opportunities for problem- solving and critical thinking. If a child is getting frustrated or disheartened, don't hesitate to help – for example by holding the creation while they attach a part.

Encourage children to find solutions when challenges arise. Support their resilience and encourage them to learn from mistakes and persevere.

Spark collaboration between children by inviting them to work together on a large or related piece. Encourage creativity and curiosity. Try saying, "Let's experiment and see what happens. Even if it doesn't work, we'll have learned something new, and we can try a different approach." The beauty of clay is that you can always roll it up and start all over again!

100 LANGUAGES

Loris Malaguzzi, founder of the Reggio Emilia educational approach, taught us how children as human beings, possess a hundred languages — a metaphor for the extraordinary potentials of children, their inner knowing and creative processes, the myriad forms with which they learn and make sense of their world.

With clay, children find a language that speaks to their innate curiosity, imagination, and desire to create. It is a language that transcends words, allowing them to express and communicate their thoughts, feelings, and ideas in a tangible and multisensory way. It is truly a gift.

NO WAY. THE HUNDRED IS THERE

The child
is made of one hundred.
The child has
a hundred languages
a hundred hands
a hundred thoughts
a hundred ways of thinking
of playing, of speaking.
A hundred always a hundred
ways of listening
of marveling of loving
a hundred joys
for singing and understanding
a hundred worlds
to discover
a hundred worlds
to invent
a hundred worlds
to dream.
The child has
a hundred languages
(and a hundred hundred
hundred more)
but they steal ninety-nine.

The school and the culture
separate the head from the body

They tell the child:
to think without hands
to do without head
to listen and not to speak
to understand without joy
to love and to marvel
only at Easter and Christmas.

They tell the child:
to discover the world already there
and of the hundred
they steal ninety-nine.

They tell the child:
that work and play reality and
fantasy science and imagination
sky and earth
reason and dream
are things
that do not belong together. And
thus they tell the child that the
hundred is not there.

The child says:
No way. The hundred is there.[3]

CLAY CREATURES

This activity offers a great opportunity for self-expression. Rather than guiding your children into making a specific animal, allow them to shape and mould the clay according to their vision of a special creature. It could be a real animal, a mythical creature, or a whimsical character straight from their imagination.

Incorporate natural materials such as sticks, rocks, shells, seedpods, or leaves. These items can become features or accessories, or tools to add texture and details.

Once the clay creatures are complete, they can be hidden in the garden for treasure hunts or used in small world play. They will become the stars of countless adventures, captivating your child's imagination for hours on end!

Things to gather:

- air-dry clay
- natural materials – sticks, rocks, shells, seedpods, leaves

Extension. Spark your child's creativity and imagination prompting them with open-ended questions such as: Where does this creature live? What does it eat? Who would the creature like to play with?

This helps children express their ideas, talk about their creative process, and often becomes a cue to extend their play and create more – a habitat or home for the creature to live in, pretend food to eat, or a playmate.

FOREST CLAY FACES

Creating forest clay faces is a fun and delightful activity that allows children to connect with the natural environment while expressing their creativity. It combines the joy of exploring the outdoors with the tactile experience of clay, plus a good dose of imagination!

To begin, take a nature walk in a forest, woods, or a park with lots of trees. Observe their different shapes, and search for natural features such as knots, burrs, hollows, and scars that resemble facial traits – can you see eyes, noses, chin?

During the walk, encourage children to gather natural materials from the forest floor, such as grasses, leaves, seedpods, and pine cones. Emphasise the importance of respecting nature by collecting resources without harming trees or plants.

Give each child an orange-sized piece of clay and have them knead it to soften it. Ask them to choose and connect with a tree and guide them to firmly press the clay onto its trunk. Using their fingers, they can shape the clay to form a face, pinch it to create a nose, chin, or ears... play with it until it begins to form into a face. Does the tree look wise? Old? Sleepy? Is it happy or grumpy?

Add intricate details to the clay faces using the nature treasures collected during the walk. Dry grasses, leaves, pine needles can become hair. Twigs can be snapped and shaped into noses and ears. Seedpods make great eyes. The possibilities are endless!

As the clay faces take form, encourage children to talk about their creations and discuss the unique qualities of each creature. Once the clay faces have served their purpose, remind children that because they used natural materials, the sculptures can be left to return to the Earth. As time passes, wind and rain will dissolve the clay, allowing it to return into the natural environment, completing the cycle of creation and transformation.

Extension. To preserve their artwork, children can draw the faces on a sketchpad or take photographs to create a visual record. Encourage storytelling and creative writing by inviting them to develop stories featuring their forest creatures. These stories can be shared and expanded upon, fostering language skills and imaginative thinking.

EASY COIL POTS

Creating coil pots is a wonderful way for children to explore clay and develop their hand-building skills. Coil pots are made by stacking and joining long coils of clay, one on top of the other – a slightly more advanced technique that allows for the creation of useful vessels and artistic objects.

Directions. To begin, help your child create a round base for the pot, measuring around 5-6mm in thickness. Using a toothpick or a butter knife, make tiny scratch marks on the outside edge of the base. These marks will help the coils adhere and join together more securely.

Next, roll another piece of clay into long coils or thick "snakes". Starting at the edge of the base, begin layering the coils around and around, gradually building up the height of the pot. Blend the edges of each coil together using your fingers or a sponge and a little water, to ensures that the coils join smoothly and stick together once dry.

Set aside to dry completely – depending on the thickness of the clay and the ambient humidity, this might take 24 to 48 hours.

Once dry, your creation can be personalised with acrylic paints or markers. Finish with a coat or two of water-resistant sealant.

STORYTELLING

THE CLAY GNOMES

Deep in the forest, not too far from here
Lies a happy little town, that's quite queer
From the outside it looks like an ordinary place
But something magical – and quite peculiar - happens in this space.

It is true that shy tiny creatures of mystical kind
Living in forests like this, you will find,
Hiding in ferns and hollows of trees,
Resting in shade of mushrooms with ease.

But in this town, there's a whole street,
Where hundreds of fairies and gnomes meet,
As the Sun sets and the kookaburra sings,
Our story of magic and wonder begins.

Long ago, on a hot summer day
The children of this town made something special to play,
They dug up clay, leaves and berries they gathered
And with their little hands this is what they created.

Chubby gnomes with hats made of nuts,
Fairies in flower gowns with mossy locks,
Nymphs dancing in waters so blue,
All made by the children, pure and true.

Each creature had a place to call their own,
In a letterbox, by the door or under a garden stone,
With comfy beds made of feathers and rock,
In gran's favourite chair, or inside an old sock.

The children were pleased, and loved their new friends
And hoped their fun would never never end
And guess what? Their wishes came true
When they're wishes of love, they always do

On every new moon, on the darkest of night
Sitting by a window the children will wait
They light up a candle and watch in wonder and awe,
As these creatures come alive without a flaw

Oh what a sight
Oh such a delight

The gnomes play, and the fairies dance,
Pixies and nymphs, in a wild trance,
From flower to flower, they frolic and play,
Leaving gold nuggets, as they make their way.

When the morning comes, and the magic fades
the grown-ups wonder at the mess that was made!

They shake their heads and are all quite confused
But the children of this street
(Who all know what happened that night)
Are all very, very amused.

MINDFULNESS

LISTENING CLAY

Time and time again I have noticed how much more relaxed and centred children appear while they work with clay. Clay slows us down and listens intently. It follows and responds to our every move. Clay demands attention and presence, often transporting us into a state of flow.

Work with clay consciously and mindfully and notice how the clay listens to your emotional and physical state of being. Invite different energies in and see how it responds. Pay attention to the sensory aspect – how does it feel on your skin, under your hands? What does it smell like?

CONNECTING TO THE ELEMENTS

Clay work is a remarkable art form that allows us to engage with the natural elements in a unique and profound way. As we mould and shape the clay, we play with the very essence of the earth, water, fire, and air, connecting with each element through the various stages of creation.

First, we touch the clay, we feel the texture in our hands. We connect with the element of **earth**, the raw material from which all life springs forth. We explore its malleability and respond to its subtle changes, allowing our creativity to flow as we shape and form our creation.

Next, we introduce moisture to the clay, the element of **water**. We feel the coolness of the clay and how it responds to our touch, becoming more pliable and receptive to our intentions. We recognise the power of water to shape and mould, just as it shapes the landscapes of our world.

As our hands work the clay, the friction generates warmth and heat. We engage with the element of **fire**, the alchemical force that brings transformation and vitality. We feel the energy radiating from our body. We understand that heat is both a catalyst and a purifier, allowing our creation to take on new forms and textures.

And finally, we surrender to the **air** element. We witness the natural process of evaporation, as the air carries away the moisture and allows our creation to solidify and take its final form.

Through this conscious connection to each element and stage of creation, our artwork becomes more than just a mere object. It becomes a reflection of our inner journey, a tangible expression of our connection to the natural world and the forces that shape and inspire us.

AS YOU WORK WITH CLAY, EMBRACE THE PROFOUND EXPERIENCE OF ENGAGING WITH THE ELEMENTS. LET THE EARTH, WATER, FIRE, AND AIR GUIDE YOUR HANDS AND IGNITE YOUR CREATIVITY. ALLOW YOUR CREATION TO TELL A STORY, TO MIRROR YOUR OWN JOURNEY, AND TO REMIND YOU OF THE DEEP CONNECTION WE SHARE WITH THE NATURAL WORLD.

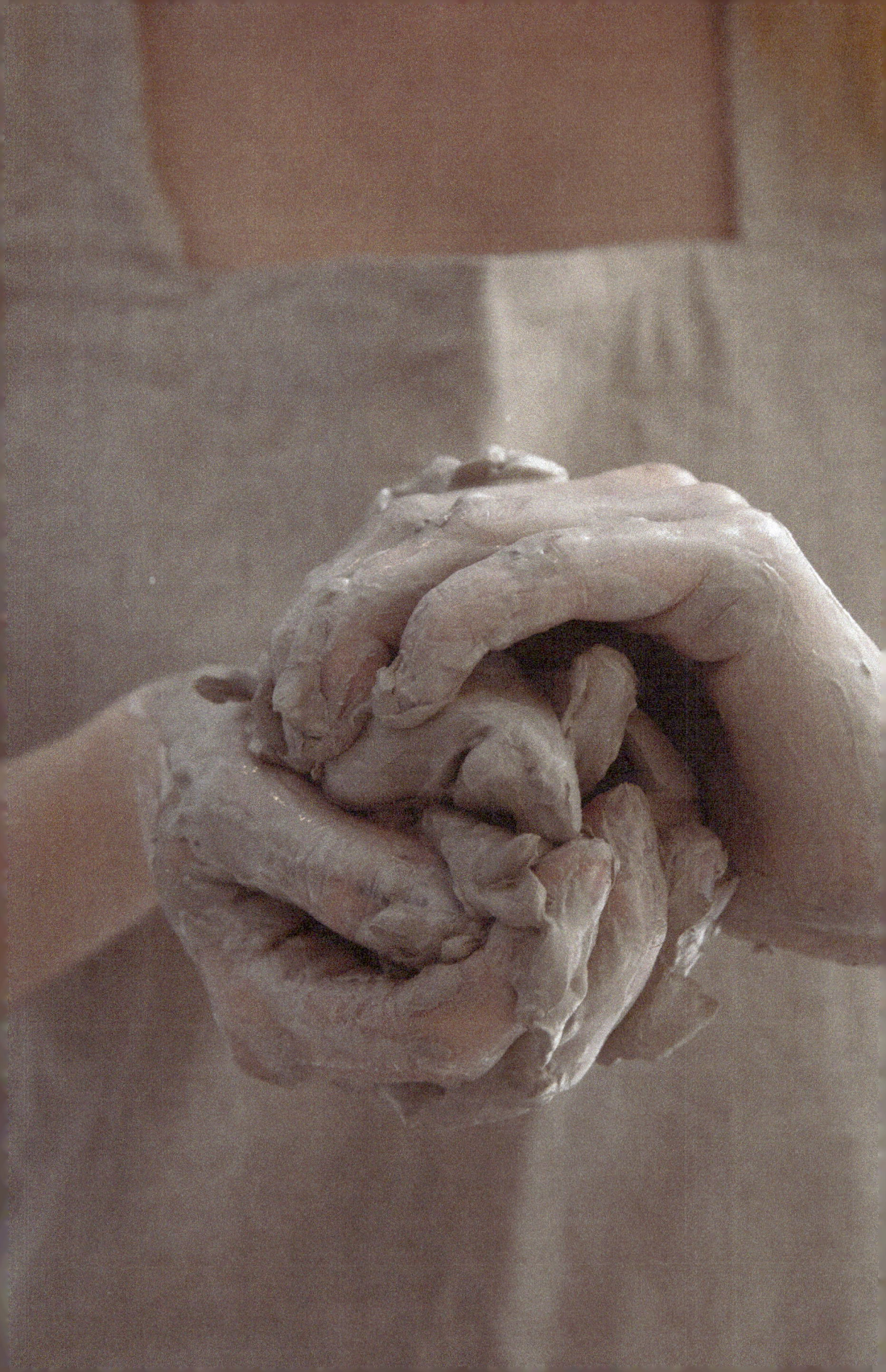

MAY

WARMING OUR SENSES

With six nimble legs, large dark eyes, and a hairy, stripey body, they quietly hum as they go about their day, collecting nectar and pollen from flower to flower. Can you guess who they are? Why, bees, of course!

On May 20th people from all around the globe celebrate World Bee Day – what a perfect opportunity to celebrate and honour these amazing insects that make life on Earth possible.

Meanwhile, autumn unfolds and we move through life with heightened awareness. Being in nature with children during this time can be a magical experience. For many creatures, autumn brings a slower pace, a time for rest and nourishment. We naturally adjust to the rhythm of the Earth.

Autumn is the perfect time to nurture our soul senses, and particularly the sense of warmth. We invite autumn into our homes with the comforting scent of spices and honey in the kitchen, sweet beeswax burning in the night, cosy blankets... simple ways to create comfort and moments of togetherness in our family.

EARTH MAGIC

BEES

You may already know that they make delicious golden honey, and soft beeswax that we can roll and mould with our warm hands. Bees are truly amazing insects, and thousands of pages have been written on their fascinating life. But, like true nature explorers, we are going to learn from direct observation – which means we are going to take a little time to watch bees and discover more about them and what they are up to.

So, grab your binoculars and let's head outside!

A WORLD FULL OF WONDER

As parents, we are blessed with the incredible privilege of nurturing our children's curiosity about the world. Understanding nature leads to respectful and appropriate behaviour, which our children observe and imitate.

Inquisitive children will naturally have questions, and it's important that we provide answers that suit their individuality and stage of development. Our goal is to build their knowledge gradually, without getting in the way of their sense of joy in discovery or limit their boundless imagination.

Below, you'll find some fascinating facts about honeybees that can enhance your observations and deepen your understanding of their behaviour. Enjoy reading them alone or with your child, but remember, don't let knowledge become a bridle to your sense of wonder. Instead, maintain a curious attitude, always open to learning and discovering more, and allow yourself to be continuously amazed.

Bees are truly captivating creatures, and, as we will learn, they play a vital role in our world. I hope this will inspire you to explore further, get closer, or simply stand back and marvel in awe, free from fear.

GETTING TO KNOW BEES

Bees are fascinating insects that live in large communities known as hives or colonies. The hive is like a big family, where every bee has a specific job. There are three types of bees within a hive: the queen, the workers, and the drones.

At the heart of the hive is the **queen bee**, the mother of the colony. She is responsible for laying thousands of eggs each day. A healthy queen will lay around 200,000 eggs in a year! Needless to say, she has little time for anything else.

The queen bee only leaves the hive once, in order to mate. For the rest of her life she will remain in the hive, while worker bees feed her continuously and look after her.

The only other time a queen bee might leave her hive is in case of a swarm. If the hive becomes too large and bees run out of space, they will make the decision to split. This is called swarming. The queen and about half the colony will eat up lots of honey to get extra energy and fly out to find a new home. A few days later, a new queen cell will hatch and she will take over the remaining hive.

Drones are the only males in a hive and their job is to find and mate with a queen bee. When they are big enough, drones leave the hive and fly to special meeting places called *congregation areas* where drones from different hives gather and wait for their chance to meet a queen.

All the while, inside the hive about 50,000 to 60,000 female bees work incredibly hard to keep the colony – their family – healthy and thriving. These are the **worker bees**.

Worker bees take on different roles throughout their lives. There are cleaner bees, whose job is to ensure that the hive stays tidy by removing rubbish, dust and debris. Nurse bees take care of the babies, feeding them and keeping them safe. Guard bees protect the hive and its inhabitants by stinging intruders. Other bees are responsible for keeping the perfect temperature within the hive: on hot days, they will stand at the front door and fan air into the hive, to cool it down. In winter months, they form a ball around the queen using their body warmth to keep her toasty.

As worker bees grow, they move to other important jobs outside the hive. They become foragers. Do you think it is exciting for a bee to venture outside of the hive?

TIME TO VENTURE OUTSIDE

Forager bees are the ones who fly out of the hive to collect nectar and pollen which they carry on their little legs like big, fluffy pants. Look up close and see if you can spot them!

When out of the hive, forager bees use a special dance language to communicate with each other. If there is a food source close to the hive, they will start a 'round' dance to call other foragers – it means, "come out, there's food here!"

If the food source is more distant, they will perform a 'waggle' dance (which looks like figure-eight repetitive movement) to exchange information on how far and in which direction they must fly to find good flowers.

It's a good day and our clever friends have found some beautiful flowers in your garden. Yum, it's a feast! Happy bees will fly back to the hive and do a little shake or tremble dance which means "There is so much nectar, more bees are needed please!"

MAKING HONEY

Nectar and pollen are used to make honey, which is bees' main source of food. Did you know that bees must visit around two million flowers to make just half a kilogram of honey? That's a lot of hard work! Luckily for us, they produce 2-3 times more honey than they need, so we get to enjoy the tasty treat too.

MORE INTERESTING BEE FACTS

- Bees are peace-loving. Only the female worker bees sting, and they only do so to defend the hive. Generally speaking, bees will pick up your vibe; if you are chilled and relaxed, bees will leave you alone. If you are tense, breathing heavily and waving your arms around looking like a bear, they are more likely to see you as a threat.
- Talking of bears... There is a reason why beekeeping suits are white – you are trying to look as little as a bear as possible. That's right. Even though they have never met a bear, European honeybees in Australia know what their most dangerous honey predator looks like!
- Bees are also amazing builders. They build their hives out of wax, which they produce from special glands in their bodies. The hive is made up of hexagonal cells that fit together perfectly, like a puzzle. This shape is very strong and efficient, and it allows the bees to store the most amount of honey and raise their young in a safe and organised way.
- Bees are very important for our environment. They help pollinate plants, which means they transfer pollen from flower to flower, helping plants make new seeds. This process is essential for many of the foods we eat, such as fruits, nuts, and vegetables.
- Recent research tells us that bees are also very clever. They can be trained to count, perform certain tasks and even recognise human faces!

I hope you'll agree with me that bees are like nature's superheroes – working tirelessly, helping plants grow and making delicious honey for us to enjoy.

So, the next time you spot a busy bee buzzing around, remember to give them a little wave and say thank you for all their hard work. Let's take care of bees by planting flowers and creating bee-friendly spaces in our gardens to help these amazing creatures thrive.

HELPING OUR BEE FRIENDS

When we care for animals and plants, something magical happens inside us. We learn about kindness, empathy, and the incredible power we have to make a difference. With our minds, hearts, and hands together, we can do amazing things!

So, are you ready to join the adventure? Here are some great ideas to get started.

Create a bee-friendly garden
Let's create a bee-friendly space bursting with beautiful flowering trees and plants. Your garden doesn't need to be big – you can start with a few pots or dedicate a sunny corner of your backyard to growing flowers. Maybe you can get your school or local community garden involved.

Flower colours that are particularly attractive to bees are blue, purple, violet, white, and yellow. Our little friends are particularly fond of lavender, bottlebrushes, and daisies, but ultimately the best flowers for your bee-friendly garden depend on where you live in Australia and what your local climate is like. Make it as unique as you are!

Set up a bee hotel
In the wild, our native bees love to nest in cosy, narrow burrows in the bush. But as our towns and cities grow, the homes of these incredible creatures are slowly disappearing, making it harder for them to find a safe place to call their own.

You can help native bees find a place to nest by setting up a bee hotel in your garden. Put on your creative hat and make one using materials you have around your home, or hop over to your local gardening store and get a ready-made one.

Men's and women's sheds as well as markets are other great places to find bee hotels.

The **Aussie Bee website** is like a treasure trove of knowledge, where you can learn all about our fantastic Australian native bees. They also have step-by-step guides that make building a bee hotel super fun and easy – check it out!

Keep it local

Let's keep the sweetness close to home by choosing Australian honey whenever possible – even better if it's from your very own local area!

By supporting local beekeepers we are not only helping the environment but also our community thrive. And you might be lucky enough to find someone who invites you to witness the incredible world inside a beehive.

Did you know?

Here are two simple things grown-ups can do to help bees:

- Mow your lawn in the evening when bees are no longer foraging.
- Encourage mixed species lawns and nature strips that include clover, dandelions and other wild flowers and allow them to flower before mowing.

EXAMPLES OF BEE HOTELS

NATURAL REMEDIES FOR BEE STINGS

Bees may have stingers, but we've learned something amazing – they don't want to harm us! Stinging is their way of protecting themselves and their hive if they feel scared or in danger.

When we are near bees, the best thing to do is stay calm and still. Never try to swat them away, as that might make them feel even more worried. We want to give them their space, just as we like our own.

When a bee stings, it usually leaves behind a barbed stinger in the skin. The stinger is what releases the venom into our body, which causes pain, itching, and swelling.

If you get stung by a bee, the first thing you should do is **check if the stinger is still in your skin** – look for a small black dot. If the stinger is still there, scrape it out with an object that is not sharp, like a fingernail, the back of a knife, or the edge of a credit card. Do not use tweezers or fingers to pull out a stinger because this only pushes more venom into the skin.

Then, **sanitise the area.** Once the stinger is out, wash the area well with soap and water. Finally, apply any of the following natural remedies:

- **Ice** – One of the simplest, yet most effective, remedies for a bee or wasp sting, ice numbs the area, reducing pain and swelling.
- **Baking soda** – Mix with water to make a paste and apply generously to the affected area to neutralise the bee venom.
- **Honey** – Kind of ironic, right? Honey can help you heal faster after a sting. Apply on the skin and cover with a band-aid.
- **Garlic** – An old folk remedy that never fails. Crush a garlic clove to release its juices, then press it against the sting site to relieve the pain.
- **Lavender essential oil** – A drop on the sting site is all you need. The essential oils in the lavender will soothe the pain and fight the inflammation.

Bee stings, although painful, tend to heal on their own without complication. Always seek immediate medical attention if you suspect an allergic reaction.

FULL MOON

HAND-ROLLED BEESWAX CANDLES

Beeswax candles are a treat for the senses, filling the air with a delicious scent that makes mealtimes, storytime, or birthday celebrations even more special. Tonight, as we celebrate the full moon, why not indulge in a magical candlelit dinner?

Things to gather:

- locally sourced beeswax sheets for candle making (A4 size)
- cotton wicks
- a sharp knife
- a cutting board
- scissors

Directions. Begin by laying a sheet of beeswax on a flat surface. Position the cotton wick along the edge of the sheet, cutting to size but leaving about 2cm to stick out.

Holding the wick in place with your fingers, start rolling the beeswax around it. The first roll should be tight enough to secure the wick – little ones might need a helping hand with this step. Continue rolling the beeswax gently, applying just enough pressure to shape the candle without breaking the sheet or damaging the pattern. As you reach the end, softly press the raw edge into the rolled candle, completing your magical beeswax creation.

Enjoy the warm glow and the sweet aroma of beeswax as you gather together for special moments with your family. Let the soft flickering light ignite your imagination and kindle precious memories.

You can cut out shapes from remaining bits of beeswax to attach to your candle or decorate with twine and dried flowers (remove before burning).

IN THE KITCHEN

HONEY CAKE

A simple cake that is deliciously moist and full of flavour.
A wildflower or orange blossom honey, sweet and floral, would work well in this recipe. Alternatively, you can add the zest of an orange to the mixture.

Ingredients:

- 2 cups all-purpose flour
- 1/2 tsp salt
- 1/2 tsp baking soda
- 1/2 cup butter, softened
- 1 cup honey
- 3 large eggs
- 1/4 tsp almond extract
- 1/4 tsp vanilla extract
- 1/2 cup sour cream or greek yoghurt
- powdered sugar, for serving (optional)

Method. Preheat the oven to 180°c and line a 9" round cake pan with baking paper.

In a large bowl, whisk together flour, salt, and baking soda. In another bowl, using a hand mixer, beat butter and honey together until the mixture is light and creamy. Add eggs, one at a time, beating well after each addition.

Next add the almond extract, the dry ingredients, then the sour cream or yoghurt and beat until it's just combined. Pour the batter into the prepared cake pan and bake for approximately 30 minutes or until a toothpick inserted in the middle comes out clean.

Be careful not to overcook this cake as it will dry up quickly. Let it cool before adding a dusting of powdered sugar. Enjoy with a cup of tea.

NATURE PLAY

HERE IS THE BEEHIVE

A fun game for our youngest explorers! All you need is a large piece of cloth – an old bed sheet or play parachute – and a few adults to hold it up. The cloth represents the 'hive'. Children follow the prompts in the *Here is the beehive* song.

HERE IS THE BEEHIVE

Here is the beehive but where are all the bees?
(Begin by holding the cloth down, all the children hiding under it)

Hiding away where nobody sees,
Here they come flying out of their hive... 1...2...3,4,5.
(Slowly lift the cloth. The children run out of the hive, buzzing like bees, following the cues)

Buzz up high *(hands up)*
Buzz down low *(go low)*
Buzzing fast *(run fast)*
Buzzing slow *(run slow)*
Buzz to the left *(all bees to the left)*
Buzz to the right *(all bees to the right)*
Buzz all day but sleep at night. *(all bees return to the hive, pretending to sleep)*

Here is the beehive but where are all the bees?
Hiding away where nobody sees,
Here they are resting inside their hive.. 1..2..3,4,5.
(slowly lower the cloth, covering the children. Enjoy the giggles.)

WILDFLOWER SEED BOMBS

Today, we become nature warriors, armed with our very own wildflower seed bombs. Get ready to spread beauty and joy to places that could use a touch of nature's magic, like forgotten corners or abandoned spaces. You will be making the world more beautiful, and the bees will be buzzing with delight and gratitude too.

Things to gather:

- flower or herb seeds
- potting soil or compost
- dried air dry clay, crushed

Directions. Let's gather our materials for the wildflower seed bombs: flower seeds like marigolds, cosmos, or sunflowers are all wonderful choices! If you've been growing these flowers at home, you can even collect their seeds from the spent flower heads.

Spread your seeds, soil, and crushed clay on a tray, and mix them together. Use equal parts of clay and compost or soil, and gently fold in the seeds. As you continue to mix, add a little mist of water, making sure the mix comes together around the seeds.

Once everything is perfectly blended, roll the mixture into little balls, each packed with the promise of blooming flowers. Find a sunny spot to let the seed bombs dry.

Finally, it's time for the grand adventure! Armed with our wildflower seed bombs, walk around your neighbourhood or school and find those places that could do with a touch of nature's brightness. There's no need to dig holes or to water them. Leave your seed balls on the ground, or throw, catapult, or slingshot them and watch as nature works its magic.

When the rain comes, the clay will dissolve, and the seeds will find their cosy spot in the soil, ready to germinate and sprout into beautiful blooms.

GIFTS TO GROW

Wildflower seed bombs make a wonderful gift. When your seed bombs are dry, wrap each one in a colourful piece of fabric or tissue paper. Place into a recycled paper envelope or gift bag and seal with a label. This is a lovely and eco-friendly gift that allows everyone to take part in helping bees.

PHOTOCOPY THE LABELS HERE INCLUDED OR DOWNLOAD THEM FROM OUR WEBSITE.

WILDFLOWER
SEED BOMBS
Plant Seeds Of Love

WILDFLOWER
SEED BOMBS
Plant Seeds Of Love

WILDFLOWER
SEED BOMBS
Plant Seeds Of Love

WILDFLOWER
SEED BOMBS
Plant Seeds Of Love

WILDFLOWER
SEED BOMBS
Plant Seeds Of Love

WILDFLOWER
SEED BOMBS
Plant Seeds Of Love

WILDFLOWER
SEED BOMBS
Plant Seeds Of Love

WILDFLOWER
SEED BOMBS
Plant Seeds Of Love

WILDFLOWER
SEED BOMBS
Plant Seeds Of Love

WILDFLOWER
SEED BOMBS
Plant Seeds Of Love

CATCHING AUTUMN COLOURS

Trees are turning gorgeous tones of yellow, orange and red right now. It's a beautiful sight! Once their colourful leaves gracefully fall to the ground, they become wonderful treasures, perfect to use in games and crafts.

So let's go on an autumn adventure! As we step outside, take a moment to appreciate the changing colours and breathe in the crisp, cool air. Our mission is to find some freshly-fallen leaves that nature has generously shared with us.

Start in your own backyard, street, or local park. Take your time as you stroll through these autumn wonderlands – you will be amazed at how nature changes and reveals its secrets throughout the seasons.

As you gather the leaves, notice how some are already displaying their beautiful autumn shades, while others are still transitioning. Marvel at the magic of this transformation and make a note of how each tree seems to have its own unique way of celebrating the season.

BEESWAX LEAVES

Autumn leaves are incredibly beautiful when they're on the tree and freshly fallen to the ground. But, after a few weeks and some rain, they start to grow mould or dry up, and their vibrant colours quickly fade away.

There is, however, a simple way to preserve the colours of autumn – by dipping the leaves in beeswax. Using this wonderful technique, your leaves will stay pliable and vibrant for months.

Use beeswax leaves on your seasonal nature table, to create an autumn mobile, decorate a window, or offer them to your child as open-ended loose parts.

Things to gather:

- a double-boiler or an old tin and a larger saucepan
- a block of beeswax, or beeswax pellets
- small metal tongs or tweezers
- baking paper
- leaves in autumnal colours

Directions. Choose leaves that are colourful and flexible. If a leaf crumbles easily in your hand, it's too dry to use. Leaves that fold gently without cracking work best for this project. Whenever possible, leave the stem attached, as it will make dipping much easier.

Now, it's time to melt the beeswax. Place some water in your pan or the bottom part of your double boiler and melt the wax slowly – be careful not to let it boil.

Once the beeswax is fully melted, carefully submerge the leaves, one at a time. All you need is a quick dip – in and out. Give the leaf a few shakes, allowing any excess wax to drip back into the pot. Lay the leaves flat on a piece of baking paper and allow to dry completely before using.

AUTUMN LEAVES MOBILE

Create a magical leafy mobile to bring the beauty of autumn into your home.

Things to gather:

- a stick
- autumn leaves – either fresh or dipped in beeswax
- string

Directions. Start by finding an interesting stick that's long and sturdy enough for this craft. Take your colourful waxed leaves and thread them onto thin string, cotton thread, or fishing line. Use small pinecones, feathers, and other nature treasures to add even more charm to your mobile. Carefully tie each item to the stick, arranging them in any way you wish.

Once your mobile is complete, hang it up in a special space where your child, and the whole family, can marvel at the wonder of nature.

LEAF RUBBING

Today we're going to explore the magic of autumn with a very special art project – leaf rubbing. The beauty of this activity is that you can experiment with leaves of all shapes and sizes and create all sorts of interesting patterns. It's a wonderful way to connect with nature and express your creativity – and never fails to amaze!

Things to gather:

- a selection of flat leaves
- beeswax crayons or oil pastels

Directions. Gather a few flat leaves from your collection. Choose different shapes and sizes. Place a leaf on your drawing board, clipboard or table, face up. Now carefully place a sheet of lightweight paper over it.

Now, it's time for the magic! Gently rub the side of a crayon or an oil pastel over the leaf, trying not to move it.

Continue until you have rubbed over the entire leaf. Make more leaf rubbings using different leaf shapes and colours.

With your collection of leaf rubbings, you can create wonderful cards to send to your family and friends, sharing the joy and magic of autumn with them.

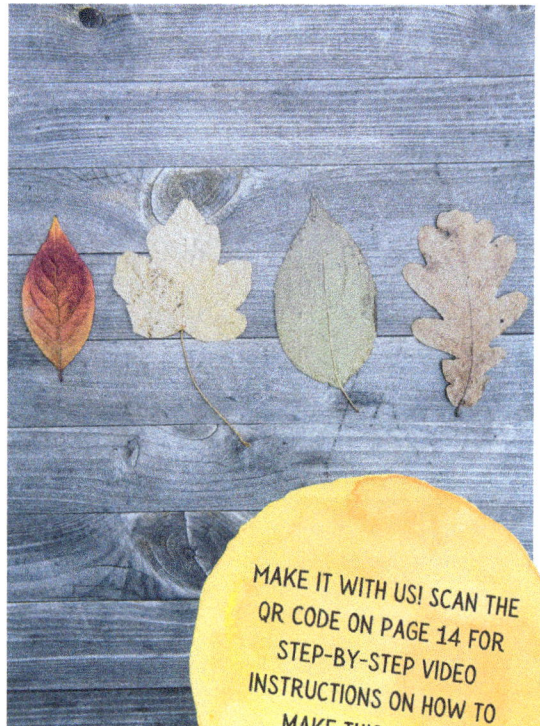

MAKE IT WITH US! SCAN THE QR CODE ON PAGE 14 FOR STEP-BY-STEP VIDEO INSTRUCTIONS ON HOW TO MAKE THIS CRAFT.

AUTUMN GAMES

Enjoy the simple pleasures of autumn with these classic games.

Catch a falling leaf
Stand under a tree and try to catch a falling leaf before it touches the ground! As simple as it sounds, it can be surprisingly tricky. Children love to play this game simply for the pure joy of jumping around.

Crunchy leaves
Dry brown leaves make a delightful crunchy noise. Go for a walk and see if you can find the crunchiest ones! Young children especially love to scrunch up leaves. Walk or jump on them, pile them up, run, roll, and dance through the leaves.

Like a leaf or a feather
This is a fun movement song. Sing together while whirling and twirling like a leaf (or a feather) until you're so dizzy you fall down!

Like a leaf or feather,
In the windy, windy weather
We will whirl around, and twirl around
And all fall down together.

Open-ended play
Leaves make a wonderful open-ended resource. You will be amazed to see how many wonderful uses your children will have for them.

MINDFULNESS

BEE BREATHING (BHRAMARI PRANAYAMA)

Let's learn the soothing art of bee breathing, a gentle technique named after a black Indian humming bee, the bhramari. This calming breath can take us to a tranquil inner space, promoting relaxation and well-being for our mind and body.

HOW TO PRACTICE BEE BREATHING

Find a comfortable seated position with your back straight, chest open, and eyes closed or gently looking downward. Use your thumbs to gently block your ears, and let your index fingers rest on your brows. Allow your remaining fingers to fall across your eyes, closing them softly.

Take a slow, deep breath in through your nose, keeping your mouth closed. As you exhale through your nose, create a long, humming sound. Feel the gentle vibration on your lips as you hum.

Continue for a few breaths. You can explore different sounds, like a buzzing bee, "om," "shhh," or "ohhh." Take a moment to become aware of how your body feels, the sense of peace and tranquillity within, and the soothing sensation of the humming.

Enjoy the peaceful journey within!

PRACTISE BEE-BREATHING WHENEVER YOU NEED A MOMENT OF CALM AND INNER PEACE. THE HUMMING WILL REMIND YOU OF THE HARMONY YOU CAN FIND WITHIN YOURSELF WHEN YOU CONNECT WITH NATURE'S RHYTHM AND EMBRACE THE PRESENT MOMENT.

Variations

- To support non-verbal children, adults can make the 'hum' sound on their behalf or use a musical instrument with a low tone.
- Younger children may need you to guide their hands over their ears until they get the idea. You can then step back and see if they can continue by themselves.
- Try doing louder, softer, higher, lower 'bee hums' together.
- Try humming along to a favourite song or rhyme. This is a great exercise for your child's vocal cords and speech muscles!

JUNE

SHINE YOUR INNER LIGHT

June sees the arrival of the colder season here in Australia and is marked by a special event – the winter solstice. The winter solstice falls in the heart of the winter season, on the shortest day and the longest night of the year. No matter where you live on Earth, and no matter what your values and beliefs are, the solstice represents a time to celebrate seasonal change.

This special festival invites us to pause amidst our busy lives, embracing the stillness and darkness, and cherishing the gifts of winter. As we gather with our loved ones, we express gratitude for all we have, and eagerly await the return of the light.

The winter solstice is a time of deep connection, uniting us with our family and friends and binding us to the Earth and its cyclical rhythms. As a family, crafting our own solstice rituals and traditions becomes a precious gift to our children.
The memories we create on these days will forever stay in their hearts – and ours.

EARTH MAGIC

WINTER SOLSTICE

A solstice is a special event that happens because of the way the Earth is tilted and how it moves around the Sun. The earliest people on Earth noticed that the Sun's path across the sky, the length of daylight, and the location of sunrise and sunset changed in a predictable way throughout the year. These changes had a profound impact on their lives, influencing important events like animal mating, crop planting, and winter preparations.

Ancient cultures built remarkable monuments such as Stonehenge, Newgrange, and Machu Picchu to track the Sun's movements. Fearing that the light would not return, they crafted special festivals and traditions to entice the Sun to rise again – the first known solstice celebrations.

Today we know that the Earth is tilted, and as it goes around the Sun, different parts of the planet get more or less sunlight, causing what we call seasons. During the winter solstice, our hemisphere is tilted farthest away from the Sun, making it the shortest day and the longest night of the year.

So, when we celebrate the winter solstice, we are celebrating the changing seasons and the beauty of our planet's journey around the Sun. But there's something else. From this moment onward, something magical happens – the days start to gradually lengthen, and the nights become shorter. From the darkest night, we slowly move into light again.

Solstice vs. Equinox
The solstice and the equinox are two astronomical events that mark the changing seasons. The word solstice means "Sun stands still" in Latin, and it happens twice a year. During the winter solstice, we have the shortest day and the least amount of daylight, while the summer solstice brings the longest day with the most hours of daylight.

Equinox means "equal night" in Latin. There are two equinoxes each year, the spring equinox and the autumn equinox, during which day and night are of equal length. The equinoxes are the only time when both the Northern and Southern Hemisphere experience roughly equal amounts of daytime and nighttime.

Upside down
It's interesting to note that when it's the winter solstice in the Northern Hemisphere, it's actually the summer solstice in the Southern Hemisphere, and vice versa. This is because the seasons are opposite on opposite sides of the planet. So, while we experience the shortest day in the north, it's the longest day in the south.

SOLSTICE MAGIC

The winter solstice is a powerful time of darkness, and darkness is often the place where magic happens. Winter is a season of stillness and rest – the plant and animal world slow down to conserve energy. It's a time for us to also slow down, go within, and find warmth in our homes and hearts.

During this potent time of transition, we can take time for introspection, reflecting on our lives, letting go of what no longer serves us, and making space for new opportunities to flow in and help us to move forward in the direction of our dreams. We celebrate our accomplishments and express gratitude for all our blessings. In the safety of darkness, we appreciate the light both around and within us.

Throughout history, the winter solstice has been a time for homecoming. People from various cultures would return to their heart's home, both literally and spiritually, to spend time with loved ones during this time. Around the world, people still light candles and bonfires, gathering, feasting, and staying up late to welcome the returning light.

When we celebrate the winter solstice, we acknowledge the importance of both darkness and light – knowing that without one, we would not fully appreciate the other.

The activities in the following pages offer simple ways to mark this special moment. Remember – it's not about how much you do, but the presence and meaning you bring to it that matters. Start simple and let the traditions grow with your family over time.

Noticing signs of the winter solstice in nature

In winter you will notice late sunrises and early sunsets, and how low the Sun appears in the sky at noon. Look at your noontime shadow – around the time of the winter solstice, it will be your longest shadow of the year! In summer it's the opposite. Dawn comes early, dusk comes late, and the Sun is high in the sky.

THE IMPORTANCE OF RITUALS

Before we dive into our winter solstice celebrations, I'd like to pause here for a moment to talk about the importance of creating meaningful traditions for our family.

When a child enters our lives, everything changes. We transition from a world of total freedom and "big things" – busy careers, wild adventures, a buzzing social life – into a world of small... small, precious moments like a little finger wrapped around ours. The excitement of a first word. Counting the hours in between feeds or sleep time. Learning about the world, one tiny step at the time.

We know that there is nothing small about these milestones. Yet, some days at home with our children can feel mundane and slow, filled with endless, repetitive tasks.

Rituals have the power to infuse seemingly ordinary moments with magic. They bring awe, gratitude, and joy to our lives. Through rituals, we can experience the journey of parenthood — and life itself — in a more inspiring and meaningful way. We become aware of deeper connections with ourselves, each other, and the natural world.

We can use rituals to express compassion, gratitude, bliss, and ecstasy. We find light as we experience the sacred and the mundane dancing together. We rediscover wonder, and suddenly, we realise that nothing is too small at all. With rituals we invite intention and attention into our world, and through repetition they become the very fabric of our life.

CONNECTING WITH NATURE THROUGH RITUALS

Connecting with nature through rituals is especially powerful. Rituals ask us to pay attention. They are so important because they can give us – and our children – a sense of identity and belonging.

While family traditions tied to holidays and celebrations are wonderful, they can come with external pressures and expectations. Creating rituals linked to nature and the changing seasons allows for a different kind of magic. We can express wonder and reverence for the universe in ways that are delightfully authentic and uncomplicated. Rituals need not be complex or time-consuming; even simple events can become sacred when experienced with presence and intention.

The process of creating a nature ritual begins with listening. Listening to our environment, our bodies, and our unconscious. As we deepen our listening, we realise that the separation between our world and the natural world is merely a human construct. Humans are not separate from nature; **we are nature.**

In essence, rituals that reconnect us with nature are really rituals that reconnect us with a more expansive understanding of ourselves.

LISTENING TO NATURE

"You know, Joe, if you or other white folks are really serious about our spirituality, you won't go asking me, or us, or anyone else about what we believe, our ceremonies, our regalia, and stuff. Instead, you will go out into the woods and talk to the sky, the earth, the rocks, the rivers, and the streams. And listen to the answers..." – Ernie "Longwalker" Peters, a Lakota Medicine Man[4]

For most of us in Australia, and depending on your latitude, temperatures are getting colder around this time of the year. Although winter officially starts on June 1st, the arrival of the cold season is a gradual and uneven process, which can't really be marked with a set-in-stone date.

But there is usually a day when you wake up and walk outside and you notice a certain smell and distinctive crispness of the air. The breeze on your skin feels cool and raw. It seems to whisper: "*Winter is here.*" Moments like these can be easily missed, like fleeting thoughts quickly swept away by the whirlwind of our minds, if we don't develop the skills of deep listening to nature.

It only takes presence of mind and an open heart to transform these observations into beautiful, simple rituals. Turn them into moments that you and your family can look forward to, year after year.

Now imagine celebrating that very first day of winter with the simple tradition of lighting a candle at the dinner table. Maybe you share a poem, a story, or blessing that reflects the mood of the season. With the anticipation of such soulful practices and moments of connection within your family, wouldn't you look forward to the arrival of the cold season?

"Because we are born from Mother Nature,
we are able to increase our life force when we connect
with her elements, cycles and rhythms.
This connection raises our vibration
and makes us become fully alive."
– Sarah Scarborough

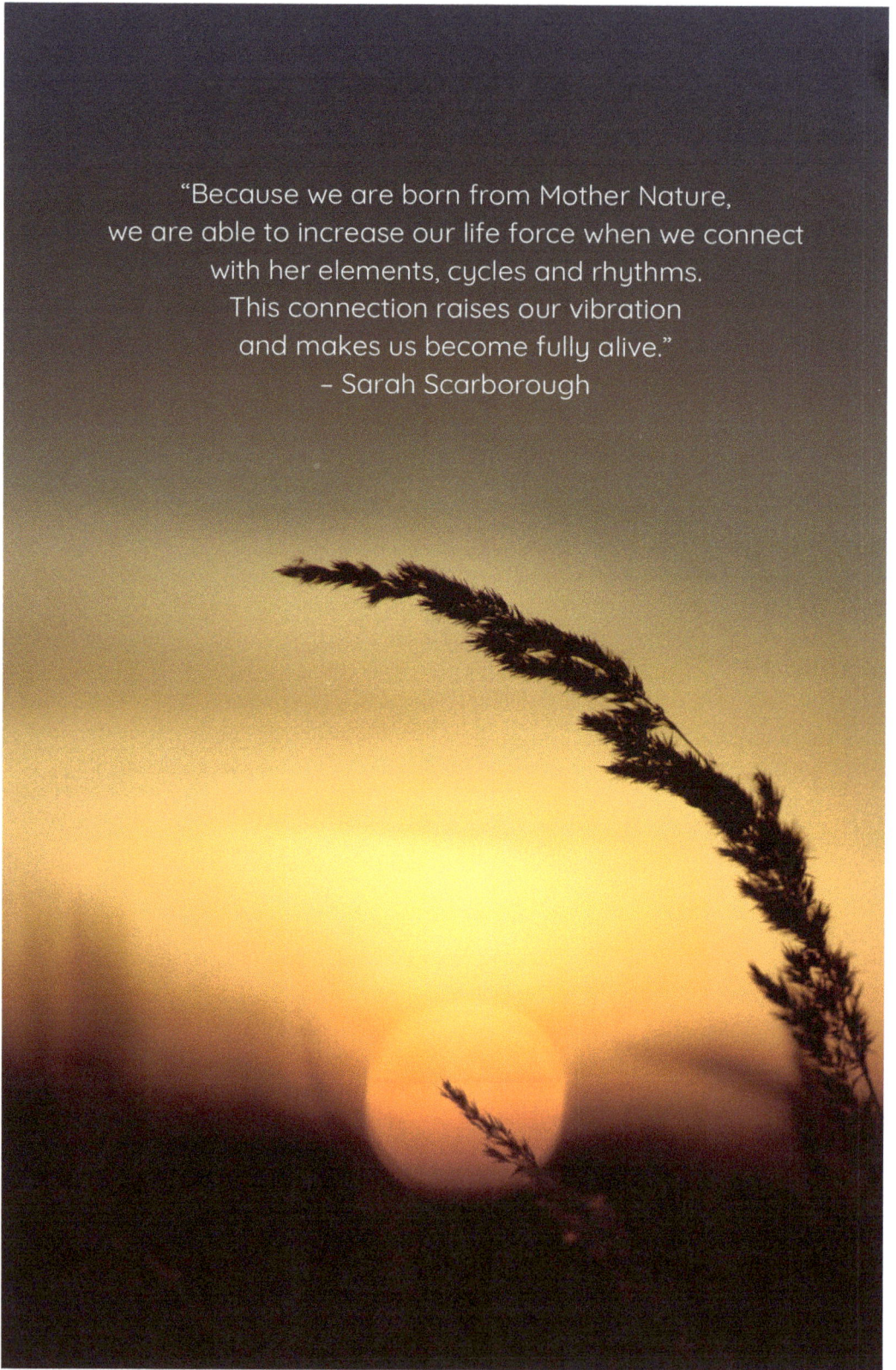

When we talk about listening to nature, we don't just mean listening to the sounds of nature with our ears. We listen with all our senses – look, smell, touch, taste (when possible). Keep a seasonal nature journal with your child and jot down what you notice. This can be done at any age: you can write, draw, or collect samples like leaves and flowers to press between the pages.

CREATING YOUR OWN NATURE RITUALS

So, you have decided to mark a special natural event – whether it's the solstice or the blooming of wattles – with a ritual. How do you decide what to do?

Rituals should arise spontaneously from our interaction with the natural world. This is when listening to our body comes in. How does the cold and darkness make you feel? What feelings, emotions or memories are stirred up by the sight of a particular flower?

By tuning in to our body sensations we can often release a surge of emotional energy. Listen carefully and with tenderness. This innate wisdom will guide you.

Rites are not invented. They are found, discovered, and experienced. From the practice of deep listening, your unconscious will give you words, music, imagery, stories, gestures which will feel especially meaningful to you.

Remember, there is beauty in simplicity. Don't over analyse it or try to create something grandiose. Even simple gestures can hold great power and depth. Standing facing the Sun, lighting a candle, pressing your palms together, or touching the Earth can be powerful components of your ritual. Trust what feels natural and authentic to you.

The act of performing a ritual can become living poetry, conveying more than words can express.

WORDS OF WISDOM

They may be your own words, or they may be the words of others – whatever you decide to bring in this sacred space, what matters is that they resonate with you and what you and your family are experiencing. Use language that your child can comprehend.

Here is a simple verse to inspire you:

I breathe in. I breathe out.
The Earth breathes in. The Earth breathes out.
This is my sacred space.
This is my heart.
This is my prayer.

MY WINTER SOLSTICE BLESSING

Write your own blessing, poem or song, or create a drawing that
represents the light in your life.

BRING THE MAGIC OF THE SOLSTICE INTO YOUR HOME

Winter may not have the vibrant colours of spring and summer, but there is still much beauty to discover and appreciate in nature.

Gather evergreen foliage like eucalyptus, tea tree leaves, westringia, or bottlebrushes, along with pinecones, which are easy to find this time of year. Arrange these treasures into circles or spirals – shapes that remind us of the cycles in nature and naturally bring us together.

Add a beeswax candle to a centrepiece for your dining table or find a corner of your home where you can create a special solstice altar.

CREATE A SOLSTICE ALTAR

You can create a special solstice altar with your family. It can be as simple or elaborate as you like, and your children will love to be part of this special moment.

There are certain elements that are particularly important to the celebration of the solstice – begin with one of these, then add more to personalise your altar:

Pinecones – Representing the spiral dance of life.
Dried sage – Supports letting go of the old and welcoming the new.
Rosemary – A sacred herb of the Sun.
Silver birch – The symbol of new beginnings.
Beeswax candles – A reminder of the life-giving force of our Sun, candles represent the return of the light.

If you love crystals, you could scatter a few around your altar. These are particularly recommended during the winter solstice:

Carnelian – A vibrant crystal that evokes the warmth of the Sun. Ancient Egyptians called carnelians "the setting sun" or the "sunset stone" because of its beautiful orange hues.

Citrine – The sunbeam crystal. Bright and yellow, citrine attracts prosperity, joy and positive energy.

Rose quartz – The stone of unconditional love, rose quartz is believed to emit strong vibrations of kindness and compassion. It is particularly beautiful to use this stone during this time of stillness and introspection.

Our winter solstice altar

CELEBRATE THE RETURN OF THE LIGHT

These simple rituals offer an opportunity for reflection and a joyful way to celebrate the return of the light with your children.

LIGHT UP THE NIGHT CIRCLE

Gather your loved ones for a joyful celebration of the winter solstice! Let's honour both the darkness and the light, inside and around us.

Things to gather:

- one large candle
- one smaller candle per person, tea lights for children, or make your own lantern
- percussion instruments: drums, pots and pans, wooden spoons, etc.
- comfortable seating for each person: cushions, sheepskins, mats, etc.

Form a circle on the floor, placing the large candle in the centre. Arrange the seats at a safe distance around it. Keep a box of matches handy next to you.

Explain to everyone the significance of the solstice – the return of the light and the beginning of a new cycle for the Earth and all of you.

Turn off all the lights and experience the darkness for a moment (children might need to feel you close – or if they're scared of the dark, keep a lit candle or a dim light near them). When you are ready, light up the candles and feel the warmth of the soft glow transforming the atmosphere.

Take a moment to appreciate the comfort of the light and the love and connection in your family and community. You can sing, dance, or use percussion instruments to make music and let go of what is no longer needed. End the ritual with a group hug or a special treat, like a cup of hot cocoa! Let the magic of this special night fill your heart with joy and warmth.

May the longtime Sun
shine upon you.
All love surround you.
And the pure light within you,
Guide your way on.

Our annual winter solstice gathering is a much anticipated event that brings
our community together. Why not create your own?

IN THE KITCHEN

SUN BREAD

Baking introduces children to the joy of making something with their own hands. Playing with the flour and the different textures is a great sensory activity. Add some measuring cups, wooden spoons and bowls and you will have hours of fun – pouring, emptying, transferring, stirring!

Ingredients:

- 3 eggs
- 3 tbsp honey
- 2 to 3 cups sifted flour
- 110g butter

- 14g instant dry yeast
- 3 tablespoons of milk of choice
- 1 teaspoon salt

Method. Stir the milk and yeast in a small bowl and let it stand for a few minutes until it foams. Mix in the eggs, honey, and melted butter. Add 2 cups of flour and finally, the salt. Knead the dough for about 10 minutes, gradually adding more flour if it's too sticky. Roll into a ball and place it in a large bowl. Cover it and let it rise for about an hour or until it doubles in size.

Divide the dough into two equal pieces. Take one piece to shape the face of the sun. Use your fingers to create eyes, a nose, and a smile. Be creative! With the remaining dough, form 10 small balls of roughly equal size. Roll them into snakes and spiral them around, like sunbeams.

Cover the bread and let it rise for another hour. If desired, brush the top with an egg wash. Bake at 200°C for 20 minutes.

Serve and enjoy warm with butter and honey.

Baking sun bread has become another lovely winter solstice tradition in our home. This is a super simple recipe, inspired by Elisa Kleven's book, and great for baking with little ones.

NATURE PLAY

SOLSTICE LANTERNS

In our family this is the winter solstice tradition we all really look forward to. There are so many ways to make lanterns – they could be as easy as decorated mason jars with a tealight inside, or as intricate as origami artwork!

Here are two simple and inexpensive ways to create lanterns, perfect for children of all ages, including toddlers.

WATERCOLOUR PAPER LANTERNS

Things to gather:

- watercolour paper (A4 or A3 size)
- watercolour paint or beeswax crayons
- paintbrushes
- olive oil
- scissors
- a hole punch, scrapbooking paper punch in different shapes or a craft knife (optional)
- some wool or string

Directions

Step 1 – Painting

- Invite your child to paint one side of the paper with watercolours or crayons, covering as much of the white as possible. Once done, brush the whole sheet with a thin layer of olive oil. This will make the paper slightly translucent (you can skip this step if you are in a pinch). Leave to dry overnight.

Step 2 – Folding
- Starting from one short end of the sheet, fold a small edge, about 2cm wide. Now fold the entire sheet in half, and then fold each half onto itself again, meeting in the middle. You will end up with four equal-sized sections and a small fold.
- Open up the paper. Now make another fold along the long edge, this time about 8-10cm wide. Create a fringe by cutting up the four creases from the bottom of the paper to the folded edge. Also, cut out the extra little bottom corner bit.
- Using a craft paper punch or a knife/scalpel with a suitable surface underneath, cut a shape on each side of the lantern – moons and stars are lovely, but simple shapes like circles and triangles would look great too!

Step 3 – Assembling the lantern
- Put the lantern together by taping the top and sides. Fold the base in and tape or glue both on the outside and inside of the lantern for added stability.
- At the top of your lantern, use a hole punch or needle to tie a string or some wool yarn. You can then tie the lantern onto the end of a long stick, like a fishing pole.
- Finally, cover the base of the lantern with double-sided sticky tape and firmly press a LED tealight onto it.

And there you have it – a beautiful watercolour paper lantern ready to light up your winter solstice celebration!

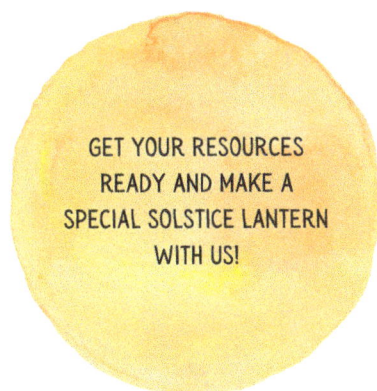

GET YOUR RESOURCES READY AND MAKE A SPECIAL SOLSTICE LANTERN WITH US!

BAKING PAPER LANTERNS

Creating lanterns with baking paper is even easier! Here's what you'll need and how to make them.

Things to gather:

- baking paper or wax paper
- a glue stick
- a selection of pressed leaves and flowers
- a round cheese box lid (or make your base with thin cardboard paper)
- scissors, hole punch
- some wool yarn, string or florist wire

Directions. Cut a sheet of baking paper, making sure it's long enough to fit around the cheese box lid, with a small overlap.

Lay the baking paper flat and make a 2cm fold along the top. Use sticky tape or glue to secure the fold in place. This will create the top edge of your lantern.

Now, it's time to let your creativity shine! Decorate the baking paper with the pressed leaves and flowers, using the glue stick to attach the natural treasures in any pattern you like.

Add some glue on the rim of your round cheese box lid and stick the decorated baking paper onto it.

Use a hole punch to make two holes on opposite sides of the lantern, on the folded top edge. Through these holes, thread wool yarn, string, or florist wire to create a handle for the lantern. Finally, place an LED tealight inside the lantern to give it a warm, inviting glow.

Bundle up and go out for a walk in the night with your lanterns!

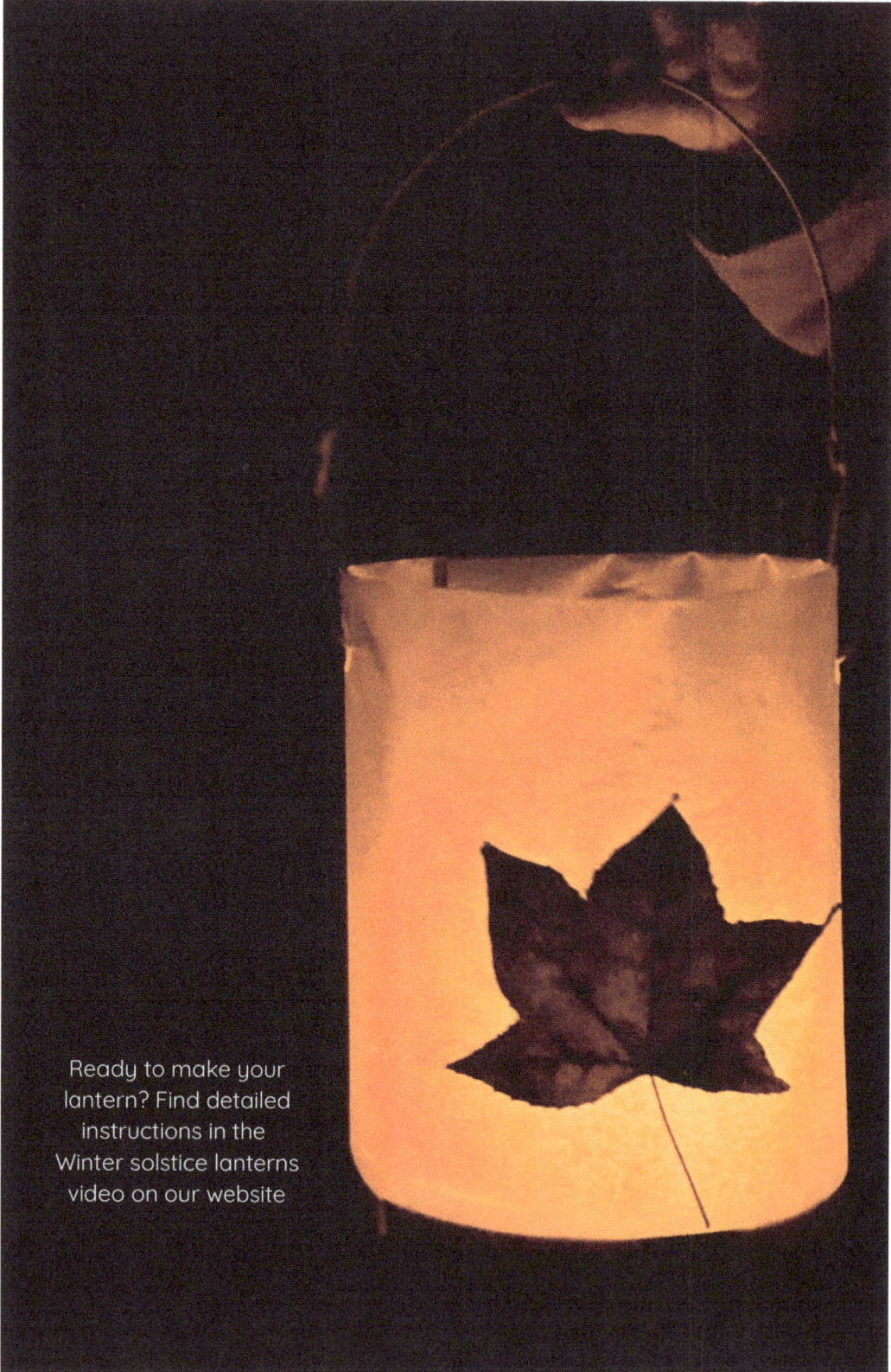

Ready to make your lantern? Find detailed instructions in the Winter solstice lanterns video on our website

TAKING CARE OF OTHERS

Most likely, you feel blessed with your life. But as we know, there are women, men, and children around us who may be lacking food, warmth, love, and safety.

Let's extend our kindness and love to those in need. Get involved with local initiatives in your neighbourhood, or participate in outreach programs, donations of food, clothes, or toys.

Encourage your child to brainstorm different ways they can spread warmth and light to people. Bake some cookies for an elderly neighbour, fill a thermos with hot tea to warm someone's night, show kindness to a stranger, say thank you in unexpected ways. Remember, no gesture is too small if it comes from the heart and brings people together.

GIVING BACK TO NATURE

Let's not forget to care for nature and the creatures that share this world with us. As winter sets in, it can be challenging for birds to find food when their usual sources like insects and berries become scarce. One beautiful way to help nature during this time is by creating seed balls for bird feeding.

By taking care of nature, we show gratitude for all the gifts it provides us throughout the year and we are reminded of the importance of giving back to the environment and all its inhabitants.

COCONUT OIL AND SEEDS BIRD FEEDERS

Birds need fat as a major energy source and to keep warm. But since they lose about 75% of their stored fat supply overnight, they need to replenish it daily. If you want to help birds during winter, you can provide them with fat-rich food in your own backyard. Here's a simple recipe that can be easily adapted with ingredients you have at home.

Things to gather:

- one part mixed bird seeds, one part oat flakes
- deodorised coconut oil
- peanut butter
- raisins, unsalted and unroasted crashed peanuts (optional)
- moulds or cookie cutters
- string

Directions. Mix seeds, oats and peanut butter together, then pour some liquid coconut oil over it. Start with one tablespoon at the time, until all the ingredients are well coated in oil.

Once you have obtained a pasty consistency, it's time to form the balls or fill moulds. Make sure to attach a string at this point by trapping it in the mixture. Then leave them in the fridge for a few hours to solidify.

Offer the seed balls in a dish on your balcony or hanging from a tree. Birds will soon be visiting you. Listen carefully as they sing "*thank you!*"

Important. Do not use flax and castor seeds as they are toxic to birds.

May the light in our hearts shine bright and remind us all of the warmth each of us brings to the world.

MINDFULNESS

FINDING STILLNESS - SIT SPOT

Sit spot is a simple mindfulness technique that allows us to truly immerse ourselves in the beauty of nature.

When we practise sit spot we sit quietly in nature, and we open our senses wide. We find a comfortable location, and return to this same spot regularly, for a chance to appreciate how that environment changes as the days and seasons shift.

Children as young as three join in this magical experience during our forest school programs. Start with just a minute or two, gently extending the time as you become more comfortable.

HOW TO PRACTISE SIT SPOT

Find a cosy spot outside, like in your backyard or at the park. Make sure you are comfortable. Sit down quietly and take a deep breath.

Now, it's time to use your special senses. Listen carefully to the sounds of nature – can you hear birds singing or leaves rustling in the wind? Feel the ground beneath you and notice if it's soft or cool. Look around with your eyes wide open. What colours do you see? Can you spot any animals or insects moving about? Inhale deeply – can you smell the grass, the mud, the flowers?

Practicing sit spot is an opportunity for being present with all our senses, and noticing what happens around us. The big, and the small things.

Try to visit the same spot regularly – it's your own secret hideout in nature. Each time you are there, you will discover something new!

JULY

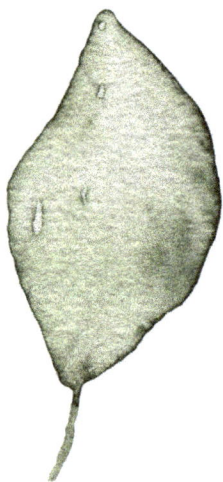

A JOURNEY HOME

The days are cool, the nights long and frosty. The Earth is resting, plants and animals already seem to be asleep... but are they? Makuru – as this season is known to the Noongar people in south-west Western Australia – is the coldest and wettest time of the year. The winds turn to the west and south, bringing the cold weather, rains and occasionally snow on the highest peaks.

Winter is also known as the fertility season – a time for a lot of animals to be pairing up in preparation for breeding. Look carefully and you will see wardongs (ravens) flying together. In lakes and rivers, black swans prepare to nest and breed. Around this time of the year, you might be lucky to spot an echidna's 'love train' – up to ten shy male echidnas, joint nose to tail, following a female for days on end... until one lucky male is finally chosen as a partner!

It is peak nectar time for honey eaters, feeding on masses of banksia flowers. In the coastal rainforests and along river banks, black bean trees (*Castanospermum australe*) are ripe and dropping their pods, gifting us a delightful supply of seed boats to float along creeks and streams.

Reptiles rest. The Pleiades, or Seven Sisters, rise in the morning sky before the Sun. This marks the start of winter and the beginning of the migration of the humpback whales from their feeding grounds in Antarctica to the warm breeding waters of northern New South Wales and southern Queensland.

Winter is probably the least beloved season for most people. Frosty mornings, numb fingers, low light. Night-time comes early and we spend more time indoors. We dream of spring, with its warmth and colours.

We can, however, appreciate this season more by understanding its role in the cycle of our lives. When we become more attuned to the changes in nature we learn to recognise the wisdom of the Earth and how it always seems to intuitively provide what our soul and body are longing for.

EARTH MAGIC

BANKSIAS

While some trees lose all their foliage and go into deep rest during winter, another plant is in full bloom. It is the time of the year when banksias put on a showy display on our eastern coastline.

Banksias have been an essential part of Aboriginal culture, serving as a significant food source and natural medicine. Honey sweet mead made from banksia flowers was offered as nourishment to young children and elderly, and used as a remedy for coughs and sore throats. The nectar dripping from the blossoms was enjoyed as a sweet treat, while the dew resting on the flowers was collected before sunrise and given to unsettled children.

The banksia plant is linked to the element of fire, and it holds magical properties of vitality, wisdom, protection, and renewal. Its leaves, flowers, and wood were used for smoke cleansing, while the cones provided fuel and were wrapped in paperbark to carry fire from one camp to the next. Interestingly, banksias propagate through fire – their seeds are released after exposure to extreme heat.

The flower heads are called spikes and consist of hundreds, sometimes thousands, of tiny individual flowers grouped together in pairs. Banksias produce creamy, yellow, orange, red, green, violet, or brown flowers.

The fruits of banksias are hard and woody follicles known as cobs. These fruits protect the seeds from foraging animals and fire. In many species, the fruits will not open until they have been burnt or completely dried out.

BANKSIA FLOWER LIFE CYCLE

Banksias go through a fascinating life cycle. The flower head starts as a cylindrical spike on the branch, appearing lime green in colour, and containing hundreds of individual flowers. As it continues to grow, it turns yellow and curves upward, forming what is known as an inflorescence.

After the blooming period, the spike starts to disintegrate, and underneath the flowers, a cob begins to grow. As the life cycle reaches its final stages, all the flowers wither away, and the spike turns into a sturdy, woody cone. The cone (cob) is made up of several capsules, which protect the seeds and open like two rounded lips when it's time for them to be released.

Can you find a banksia tree near you and observe the various stages of its life?

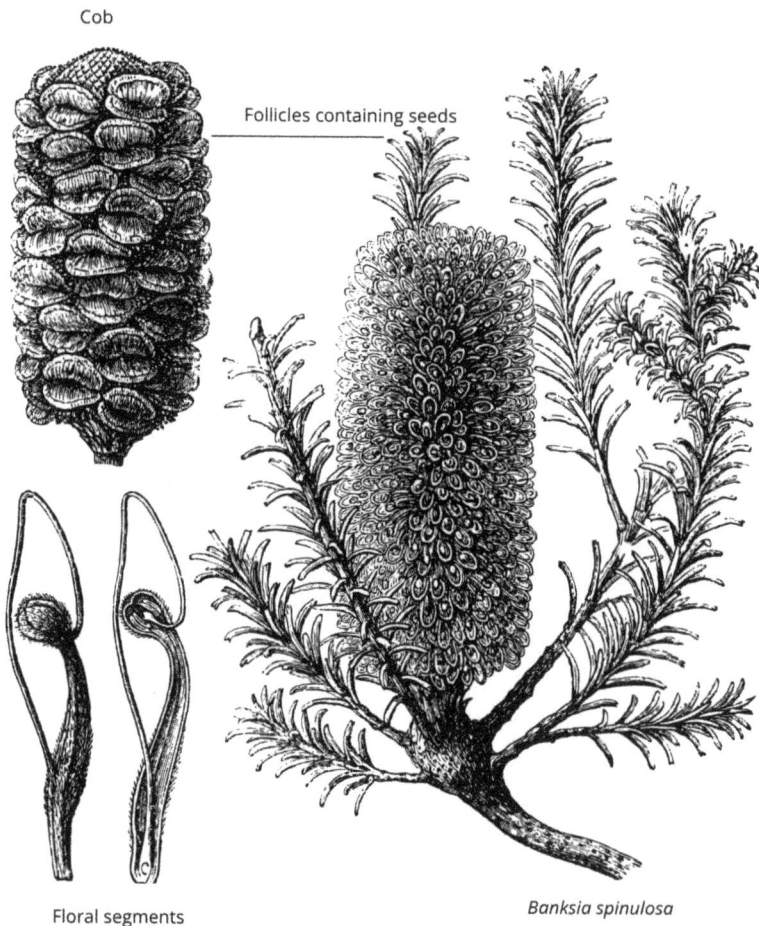

Cob

Follicles containing seeds

Floral segments

Banksia spinulosa

AN IMPORTANT FOOD SOURCE

Banksias play a vital role in the Australian bush food chain. They offer a rich source of nectar, serving as nourishment for so many creatures. Our birds are particularly fond of this native plant.

For example, the seeds and larvae found inside the banksia cob follicle provide great sustenance for cockatoos. Lorikeets and silver-eyes, which are nectar-feeding birds, have developed an incredible ability to track the flowering seasons of various banksia species. Honeyeaters have a unique and fascinating connection with banksias – did you know that the shape of the banksia flower matches perfectly with the shape of their tongue, allowing them to access the nectar easily?

These remarkable plants are not only beautiful and ecologically important – they play a significant role in helping many animals survive and thrive in their natural habitats.

Can you recognise different species of banksias? Photocopy the banksia identification cards on the next page or download a copy from our website and see how many you can find in your local area.

COASTAL BANKSIA
Banksia integrifolia

The underside of the leaves has a distinctive silver-white colour which shows up when coastal breezes blow. Nectar rich flowers in winter, loved by bees!

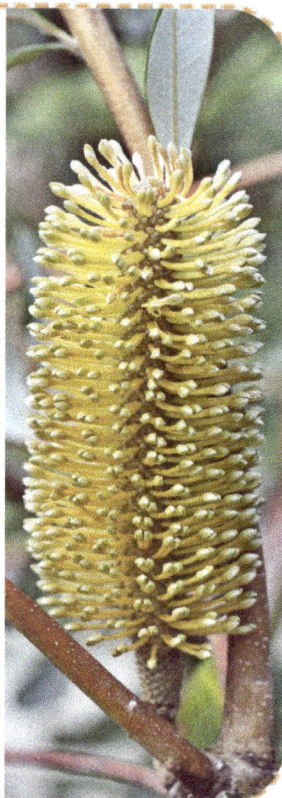

HAIRPIN BANKSIA
Banksia spinulosa

Long orange, red and gold flowers. Leaves are long and narrow. The trunks have smooth, grey-brown bark.

SWAMP BANKSIA
Banksia robur

This bold rugged banksia is often found near ponds and creek banks or along river margins. When in bud, flowers appear as a bluish green but turn yellow-green as the flowers open.

OLD MAN BANKSIA
Banksia serrata

Named after their distinctive wrinkly grey bark and gnarled shape. They have shiny dark green leaves with saw-toothed edges. As these flowers age, the flower spikes turn grey, then develop into large brown-grey woody seed pods

Banksia cobs are fantastic loose parts. They create interesting patterns when rolled over clay or playdough and make for great critters!

MAKING BANKSIA FLOWER ESSENCE

Making flower essence with banksias is a special way to capture the magic of these beautiful plants. A flower essence is a water infusion that harnesses the Sun's energy to extract the essence (or life force) of a plant and transfer it into the water. Flower essences are a type of vibrational medicine, primarily used to support our emotional, mental and spiritual well-being.

Making flower essence at home can be a joyful and a deeply meditative experience. Carefully picking each flower as they get kissed by the first morning sun. Watching them float in spring water. Setting an intention.. There is so much love that goes in the process!

Flower essences have a gentle energy and are safe for everyone – adults, children, pets and even plants. Here's how you can make your own.

Things to gather:

- fresh banksia flowers
- a glass bowl
- spring water

Directions.
Connect to the flowers
Gather the flowers in the morning – the earlier the better. The morning dew on the flowers is thought to bring the most beneficial effects. Try to be present and feel the energy of the plant. Make sure you pick them from a place where they grow in abundance and are not exposed to pollutants.

Let the Sun work its magic
Place the flowers in a clear glass bowl filled with spring water. Leave the bowl outside in direct sunlight for a few hours. The Sun's energy will transfer the essence of the flowers into the water.

Create the mother essence
After a few hours, remove the flowers from the water – if possible, using a leaf from the plant. This is called the "mother essence." Pour it into a clean, amber glass jar or bottle and mix it with an equal amount of brandy or glycerine to preserve it.

Label the bottle, with the name of the flower, date, place and store in a cool, dry place. If stored correctly, mother essences will retain their potency for years. If using glycerine instead of brandy, however, keep it in the fridge and use it within one year.

Make stock bottles
The mother essence is never to be taken directly - we need to dilute it first.
Fill another bottle with half water and half brandy and add 5-10 drops of mother essence. This is your stock bottle.

How to use
You can use the flower essence in different ways. Put 3-5 drops directly in your mouth or mix with water, three or more times daily. Spray it in your room, or add a few drops to your bath for a beautiful and relaxing evening routine.

FULL MOON

THE ORIGIN OF THE MOON

In July, Indigenous and non-Indigenous communities all over Australia celebrate NAIDOC Week – an annual event that honours the history, culture, and achievements of Aboriginal and Torres Strait Islander peoples. So it seems fitting to share this beautiful Dreaming story from Cape York, in far northern Queensland, on how the Moon came to be.

"Many years ago, people realised that a light was needed at night time because they found it difficult to walk around or to hunt. The Sun lit up their daytime – something was needed to light up the night. They held a big meeting, and one idea was to collect a huge pile of firewood during the daytime hours and setting fire to it just as the Sun set. People thought that the fire would be big enough to light up the bush so that they could hunt and walk around and have corroborees (gatherings). Most of the people thought that this idea was impractical.

One member of the tribe had a great idea: Why not make a special boomerang that would shine, throw it high into the sky and at night this boomerang would give enough light to allow people and animals to see at night?

They made a giant boomerang. People tried to throw it high into the sky. They tried but they just couldn't throw it high enough. Then, a very thin, old, weak man stepped forward and politely asked if he could try. Everyone laughed at him when they saw his weak, thin arms. One of the elders was a kind and wise man and he said the old man should be allowed to throw the boomerang.

And throw the boomerang the old man did! It went higher and higher and higher and finally stayed up in the sky as the Moon, shining down onto the people."

– Australian Indigenous Astronomy[5]

MAKE A BOOMERANG FOR THE FULL MOON

Traditionally, boomerangs were made using a curved piece of wood, usually from the section where the tree trunk joins a large root, making an angle. They were then heated over a fire and further bent to achieve the right wing angle.

Making a functional boomerang is a beautiful craft but today we will have some fun creating a symbolic boomerang for the full moon using poinciana seed pods.

Things to gather:

- poinciana seed pods
- acrylic paint
- q-tips, a round tip brush or paint brushes

Directions. Look for a curved poinciana seed pod – they come in many shapes and sizes, some of them really resembling a boomerang.

Open it up, remove the seeds and give it a good clean. Decorate your boomerang with paint. If you want to try dot art, you can use brushes, small twigs or q-tips.

Once the paint dries, head to a large open space and try it out!

NATURE PLAY

WINTER TREES

You might have noticed that some trees stay green all year round, while others lose their leaves in autumn. The ones that lose their foliage are called deciduous trees. Some well-known deciduous trees in Australia are flame trees, jacarandas, silver birches, frangipanis, and red cedars.

Without colours, and bare of their leaves, these trees may seem dead, but they are actually just resting. They had all autumn to enter this phase peacefully and gradually, and now they are in a state called *dormancy*. Cold temperatures slow down their mechanisms – the trees are still living and growing, only in slow motion.

And since nature has thought of everything, the leaves that fell off in autumn now create a protective layer on the ground, like a cosy blanket keeping the roots safe from frost.

ADOPT A TREE

Find a tree that lives near you and that you feel drawn to – we will spend some time connecting with it. Let's begin by observing it closely. Is the tree shedding its bark? Is it an evergreen, with leaves that stay green all year round, or is it a deciduous tree?

Take a moment to explore the area right under the tree. What do you see there? Are there fallen leaves? Any interesting plants or fungi growing?

Next, look at the twigs of the tree and see if there are any buds on them. Buds are small growths on the branches that will eventually turn into new leaves or flowers.

Now, let's use our sense of touch to feel the tree's bark. Is it rough or smooth? Run your fingers along it and describe how it feels.

Lastly, use your sense of smell. Do you notice any particular scent? Some trees have a very distinctive smell, often used to communicate with other trees and creatures.

Make sure to record all your observations in your nature journal. You can write down what you noticed or even draw pictures. This way, you will be able to keep track of the changes in your tree over time and learn more about it.

MAKE AN OFFERING

With less sunlight available in winter, your special tree will love some extra nourishment and attention from you. A good and easy way to do this is to make an offering of oatmeal – simply sprinkle a little bit of oats around the trunk of your tree or plant. Oats are a nutritious food not only for us people, but also for trees and plants. They contain nitrogen, phosphorus and potassium, and are particularly high in phosphorus, which helps roots to grow. Of course, while you are there, you can also give your tree a big hug, sing to it or say thank you!

DECORATE YOUR TREE

Show your love and appreciation for your adopted tree by creating some colourful decorations to brighten up its bare branches.

Things to gather:

- ribbon or string
- scissors
- a selection of twigs, leaves, dried fruit, nuts or feathers
- coloured wool and beads

Directions. Use the natural treasures you gathered to make some lovely decorations. You can wrap colourful wool around them, create mobiles or paint them. Let your creativity flow! Another fun idea is to learn how to make a God's Eye (find the video on our website). Choose a branch and carefully tie or hang your creations on your special tree.

LEARN HOW TO MAKE GOD'S EYES – BEAUTIFUL TRADITIONAL ORNAMENTS MADE WITH STICKS AND YARN.

MAKE YOUR OWN ADVENTURE BINOCULARS

Calling all young explorers...The humpback whales are on their way to Australia! It's time to make your very own binoculars and embark on exciting whale watching adventures. Not only is this a fun project, but it's also a great way to reuse empty toilet paper rolls. Win, win!

Tip. If you want to use the binoculars to see things up close, use a hot glue gun to add in magnifying glasses as the lenses.

Things to gather:

- 2 empty toilet paper rolls
- white glue
- string or ribbon
- construction paper, butcher paper or coloured felt sheet
- washi tape (optional)
- decorating supplies – markers, crayons, or tissue paper

Directions. Wrap construction paper around each toilet paper roll and secure it with tape. You can also leave them bare or decorate them with crayons – your choice!

Glue the two toilet paper rolls together, making a binocular shape. Take another piece of construction paper or felt and wrap it around the two rolls to hold them together. Secure the ends with tape.

For extra flair, add washi tape to both ends of the rolls, and use stickers or crayons to decorate the binoculars. Poke holes on the sides and thread a string through them to create a strap. Skip this step if the binoculars are for a younger child.

Your DIY binoculars are now ready! Head outside and test them out. How far can you see? Have fun exploring the world around you.

HUMPBACK WHALES

During winter, our coastline becomes alive with the arrival of the magnificent humpback whales. Time to pack up our binoculars and head out to enjoy one of the greatest shows on Earth!

Every year, thousands of humpback whales undertake what is known as the world's longest mammal migration. They leave the freezing waters of Antarctica and journey to the warm waters of Australia for mating, giving birth, and nurturing their newborns. As they leave Antarctica, some of them swim around Tasmania and head up the east coast to Hervey Bay in Queensland, while the rest travel up the west coast of Australia to places like Broome and the Kimberley.

The timing of their arrival in Australia depends on the temperature of the water, among other things, but it generally occurs between March and May each year. Many communities around Australia celebrate this time with welcoming of the whales' ceremonies.

July to September is the main mating time, and the male whales put on quite a show to attract the attention of females! Pregnant mama whales also give birth during this period.

The calves grow rapidly, doubling in size from around four metres at birth to eight metres in just three months. Which is no surprise, since they drink up to 500 litres of their mother's milk each day. This quantity is so enormous it is difficult to imagine!

The mothers, instead, haven't eaten since leaving Antarctica, so, as soon as the calves are strong enough, usually around September, they start their journey back to their feeding grounds, where they will find an abundance of krill.

Mothers and calves swim together, often closer to shore to stay safe from predators. It's the perfect time for whale watching!

WHAT CAN WE DO TO PROTECT OUR WHALES?

Australia's humpback whale population has increased from an estimated critically low 200 animals in the 1960s to around 60,000 now (and still growing) following the whaling ban in 1978. This is wonderful news.

But there is still so much more we can all do to protect our whales and all marine creatures. Here are some ideas.

Learn about whales and spread the love
Learn more about these amazing creatures. Explore books, videos, or visit websites. Follow their journey using our humpback whales migration calendar (also available to download on our website).

Do not disturb
Watching whales and dolphins in their natural environment is an exciting and rewarding experience but let's always keep a respectful distance. If you're on a boat, don't get closer than 100 metres to a whale or 50 metres to a dolphin. Remember that animals need to rest, and disturbing them can be harmful.

A humpback whale with her newborn calf wallowing in the protection of a sheltered bay is resting. If you approach too closely, she will be keeping a watchful eye on you and may suddenly try to defend herself or go somewhere else, using up much needed energy reserves. Similarly, if going on a whale watching tour, do your research and make sure you engage a thoughtful and responsible company.

Also, remember that observing whales from the coastline can be just as exciting!

Say no to plastic
Plastic pollution is a major threat to all marine life. To save whales for future generations, we need to prevent plastic from entering the ocean – plastic bags, plastic packaging, plastic sheets, fishing rope, nets, tackle, and balloons are all big hazards in the water.

Participate in beach clean-up days or create your own to keep your local beach clean and plastic-free. Even better, whenever possible say no to single-use plastic all together.

Support those working to protect the ocean and marine wildlife
Organisations such as Australian Marine Conservation Society (www.marineconservation.org.au) and Sea Shepherd (www.seashepherd.org.au) are a great place to start. You can volunteer for them, get your school, family and friends involved in some of their initiatives or support their work through a donation.

Humpback whales have extraordinary navigation skills! They travel thousands of miles deep underwater, following pretty much a straight line and without getting lost. Some scientists believe that they use the Sun, the Moon and the stars to find their way.

HUMPBACK WHALES MIGRATION CALENDAR

Follow the journey of these playful creatures as they travel along Australia's eastern coastline

DECEMBER - FEBRUARY

Feeding in the Antarctic

Humpbacks spend most of their time feeding on krill and building up their fat stores (blubber) which will sustain them during the long migration

FEBRUARY

Northerly migration begins

The world's longest mammal migration begins – a 10,000 km journey to the warm waters of Australia where humpbacks mate, calve and nurture their newborns

MARCH

Migration is well under way

First sightings in southern Tasmania

APRIL

Pregnant females follow

Females stay in the Antarctic feeding for longer to build up stocks to support themselves and their young on their long journey

MAY

Whales arrive off mainland Australia

Time to grab your binoculars in NSW!

JUNE - JULY

Heading to Queensland

Time to grab your binoculars in QLD!
Whale watching tips:
be patient - be respectful - keep your distance

JULY - SEPTEMBER

Mating time

Males show off breaching, tail slapping and singing to attract females

JULY - AUGUST

Pregnant females give birth

New calves are born in the warm waters of the Great Barrier Reef

SEPTEMBER - OCTOBER

Spot the newborn calves

Mothers and calves swim close to the shore to keep safe from predators. Calves drink around 250 litres of their mother's milk per day and grow at an astonishing rate

OCTOBER

Time to head back south

It's almost time to say goodbye to our friends.
Calves are now strong enough to face the journey, so humpbacks head back south

NOVEMBER

Back in the Southern Ocean

The last sightings are around Eden, NSW and Tasmania at the end of November

DECEMBER

Feeding in the Antarctic

Humpbacks are finally back in the Antarctic, where they feast on krill and stock up on blubber reserves before their next migration north

© Big Scrub Nature Play
bigscrubnatureplay.com

LEARN THE LANGUAGE OF THE WHALES

Have you ever wondered why whales behave in a certain way? Read on to learn how they communicate and the meaning of certain behaviours.

Fluke
The whale lifts its fluke (or tail) out of the water before diving, in order to descend steeply beneath the surface.

Blow (spout)
As whales reach the water surface to breathe, they forcefully expel air through the blowhole. As warm air from the whale's lungs meets cold air outside, it condenses into a cloud, like seeing your breath on a cold day.

Spy hop
The whale lifts its head out of the water. Whales may spy hop out of curiosity, especially if a boat is around. *Hello, who's up here?*

Breach
Breaching is another form of communication for whales. It is believed that all slapping creates sounds used to send messages to other whales, and the big splashes are for sending messages long-distances.

Tail slapping
The whale slaps its fluke to the surface. High energy tail slapping is a way to signal danger and warn off predators.

Happy whale watching!

STORYTELLING

THE WHITE WHALE

It was a warm winter day, and the ocean was beaming with life. Dolphins were riding the waves, gannets were plunging into the water in search of food, and whales were swimming inside the bay.

The whales were very happy and playful. Every now and then, one of them would dive deeper and then suddenly pick up speed and burst out of the water, in a great jump, creating foam and bubbles, and making a loud, smacking sound. *Splash!*

There was one whale within this pod, however, who was very quiet and keeping a distance. She was about to give birth. Only moments later, a calf gently floated out of her body and into the water. The calf and the mama started swimming together in a graceful dance of love – eyes shining with the excitement of finally meeting one another.

The calf was healthy, and hungry already. After floating to the surface for his first breath, he started searching for milk. It was only at this point that mama whale noticed something peculiar. Her baby was not black or grey, like all the other whales and like herself, too. He was white. Entirely white. Not a hint of colour on his long body.

Soon, the other whales arrived and they were all so surprised to find a white calf. Not everyone was kind. Some of them laughed, others said that he could not be part of their pod, for it was far too dangerous to have a white whale with them.

Mama whale felt sad, but she did not care about what the others said or thought. She loved this calf so deeply. She began to sing a beautiful slow song. The calf could not understand it yet, but he loved his mama's voice – it was the most beautiful sound in the ocean.

Meanwhile, news of the white whale spread quickly over the land and the ocean. One day, as mother and baby were swimming together, they found themselves surrounded by boats. The people on board were shouting, pointing. They kept coming closer and closer, until they could almost touch the whales. They all wanted to see the white calf.

"Migaloo" – the mama whale heard them say. "White fella."
White fella... Migaloo... She realised they were calling her baby.

The mother covered Migaloo with her long body, trying to protect him, but the people would not go away. So she did the only thing she knew – with all the strength that she could find in her body, she slapped her huge tail. Once... twice... three times. The slaps created big waves in the ocean, the boats started rocking wildly, and the people finally left them alone.

Over the next few days more people came, but they had learned their lesson. They knew they had to be gentle and kind, and so they kept a distance from Migaloo, admiring his white shimmering body from afar.

Migaloo was growing quickly – every day getting bigger and stronger. His mother had been singing to him about the long journey they were about to embark on. Soon they will start swimming together and they will not stop for months, until they reached Antarctica – a land of snow and ice and food, so much food for hungry whales like Migaloo!

"One day, my dear Migaloo" – she would say – "you will be on this journey on your own. But for now, it is you and me. Together, taking care of each other."

Year after year, Migaloo returns to Australia and people from all over the world come to see him. They cheer and clap for him at every jump, sometimes even follow him for days. Migaloo knows they are there to protect him. He does not mind being different from the other whales anymore. His white skin turned out to be a blessing – a gift from the ocean.

Maybe one day, as you are sitting on a quiet beach, watching the whales travelling along, you will see a splash. And bursting out of the water there will be a white whale, his long body shimmering in the sun like a cloud.

And you will know that Migaloo is out there, saying hello.

STORY STONES

Make your very own mama whale and baby Migaloo story stones. Add more stones to expand your collection as your child's imagination grows!

Things to gather:

- two medium-sized stones
- paint or paint pens
- modge podge or water-based sealer (optional)

Directions. Search for medium-sized stones either at home, in nature, or in a craft or landscaping shop. Look for stones with a relatively smooth surfaces and that can lay flat, as it will make the painting process much easier. Once you've found your stones, give them a nice wash in hot, soapy water and let them dry completely before painting.

You can sketch the outlines of your whale pictures with a pencil first, but don't worry about perfection. Remember, story stones are all about sparking the imagination, so let your artistic spirit soar!

Use paint or paint pens to bring your whales to life. Children can paint their own story stones or help by creating the ocean background. This is a great opportunity for some beautiful collaborative art.

Allow your painted stones to dry completely. Once the paint has set, you can apply one or two coats of mod podge or a similar water-based sealer. This step is optional, but it will help protect the paint, preventing it from fading or chipping, and ensuring your story stones remain vibrant for many storytelling adventures to come.

Place the stones in a special container or pouch. Let your imagination guide you through the deep blue sea, where Migaloo and his mama swim gracefully and happily together.

AUGUST

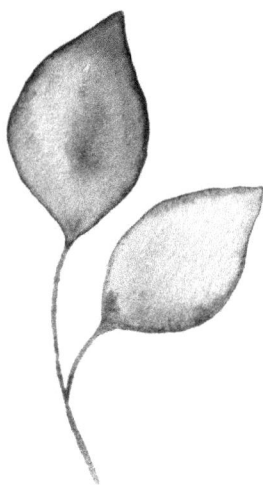

JOYFUL TRANSITIONS

The weather becomes dryer and slightly warmer as August arrives, bringing with it the strong westerly winds. As the season transitions, echidnas and turtles emerge from hibernation, basking on warm logs, a clear sign of changing weather.

The world of birds becomes a flurry of activity as many prepare to build their nests and gear up for breeding season. Magpies engage in song battles, trying to secure territorial patches that include suitable trees for nesting.

The male superb fairy-wrens display their iridescent blue breeding plumage, hoping to capture the wandering eyes of the females. Meanwhile, black cockatoos are scouring the landscape in search of wood grubs.

Amidst the greenish-grey of the winter landscape, masses of vibrant yellow flowers brighten the sky – it's the season of wattles. Nearly one-third of Australia's 960 wattle species will bloom during this time, filling the air with their delightful scent and the promise of an approaching spring.

EARTH MAGIC

WATTLES

The bush suddenly glows with golden light. Bursts of brilliant yellow flowers light up the whole canopy, filling the air with the sweetest fragrance. It seems to happen almost overnight: One day the landscape feels bleak and quiescent and the next, wattles are in full bloom.

Wattle trees are unruly, untameable, strikingly beautiful, and yet so unpretentious – they perfectly embody the spirit of our country. Not surprisingly the golden wattle (*Acacia pycnantha*), is Australia's floral emblem and the inspiration behind our national colours, green and gold.

Wattles are a common sight in many parts of Australia, adorning the landscape with their brilliant hues of yellow, gold, and sometimes cream or white. The flowers typically appear in late winter and spring, blooming along the coast first and then gradually inland. After the tree has finished flowering, curly seed pods appear containing wattleseed – a bush delicacy!

Did you know?
Wattle = Acacia. Wattle is the common name and Acacia is the scientific name for what is largest genus of flowering plants in our country. Did you know there are almost 1000 species of Acacia in Australia? Each species has a common name and a unique scientific name. For example:
Acacia melanoxylon = Blackwood wattle
Acacia pycnantha = Golden wattle
Acacia aneura = Mulga wattle
Acacia fimbriata = Brisbane wattle.

WATTLES AND WILDLIFE

Wattles attract and provide sustenance for so much wildlife! Here are some fascinating facts about their relationship with various creatures:

- The first wattle blooms are a sign that the burri burri (whales) are on the move.
- So many birds are fond of wattle seeds: red-tailed black cockatoos, crimson rosellas, red wattlebirds, superb fairy-wrens, various honeyeaters, king parrots and silvereyes. Can you spot any of these birds on wattle trees near you?
- Yellow-tailed black cockatoos use their massive beaks to rip open the wood of wattles to expose and eat the grubs that live within it – they consider it a delicacy!
- When flowering, wattles produce a sugar that attracts ants, native bees and wasps.
- There are twenty three species of wattles that serve as host plants for the Imperial blue butterfly, playing a crucial role in its life cycle.
- The copious amount of pollen produced by wattles is an important source of protein for bees during the winter months, when there are fewer plants blooming and therefore less food available.

POLLINATION

The way wattle flowers pollinate is very fascinating. Unlike other plants whose lightweight pollen is easily carried by the wind, wattles produce large and heavy pollen grains. For this reason, these trees largely rely on insects for pollination.

Whenever insects like bees, wasps, and beetles land on wattle flowers to gather nectar, they also become coated with pollen. As they move from one plant to another, they transfer the pollen, allowing for cross-pollination. This clever strategy ensures that wattle trees can reproduce and thrive.

OBSERVING

Find out which wattles grow in your area. Visit these trees regularly and record your observations in your nature journal. Note blooming periods, the appearance of seedpods, and any fascinating interactions between wattles and wildlife. Observe the different insects that visit the flowers, such as bees, butterflies, and ants. What are they doing?

Can you spot any caterpillars? They are most likely Imperial blue butterfly caterpillars, which exclusively feed on wattles.

The females of the imperial blue lay their white-greenish eggs on the stem of the plant – but before they do that, they make sure the tree has the right type of ant colony. If you look up closely you will most likely see the caterpillars surrounded by ants. This is because the caterpillars secrete a substance that ants love. In return for this tasty treat, the ants offer protection from predators. How remarkable!

ABORIGINAL USE OF WATTLES

Wattle has long been valued as a source of food and medicine, and for the quality of its timber, which was used to produce tools, weapons and musical instruments. These are some of the ways Indigenous Australians have been using wattles.

Nourishment
Seed pods were harvested, roasted, and eaten whole, or ground into a flour or paste like peanut butter. Wattle seeds are a great source of protein and can be stored for long periods of time. Only the seeds of certain varieties can be eaten like the mulga (*Acacia Aneura*). The sugary gum from the tree was eaten raw or dissolved in water to make a sweet drink.

Healing
Medicinally, wattles were used to treat headaches, skin issues, aches and pains, infections, colds and toothaches. Leaf stems, bark and roots were infused and applied topically or drunk to treat different ailments.

Smoke treatment was also widely used. People would sit around the fire and inhale the smoke produced by the burning of leafy branches of wattle. Mothers and their newborn babies would sit in the smoke produced by the mulga wattle to promote good health in the child and to speed the mother's recovery.

Utensils
The wood from wattles was used to produce hunting spears, boomerangs, clap sticks and fire drills, amongst many other things.

FULL MOON

MOON WATER

Full moons mark intense moments of culmination, radiating light and vibrant energy. Creating moon water is a delightful and child-friendly ritual that allows us to harness and amplify this celestial energy in our lives.

What is moon water? As the name suggests, it is water that has been basking under the luminous glow of the full moon, absorbing some of its potent power. During this phase, the Moon shines brightly, and this month, we want to invite in the vibrant, joyful energy of the wattle too, using this opportunity to celebrate all the things that fill us with love and light.

HOW TO MAKE MOON WATER

Fill a jar or bowl with filtered water. Add wattle flowers to it, then place the container outside or on a windowsill, directly in the moonlight's path. Let it sit overnight. For added celestial energy, you can place crystals on top of the jar or around the bowl, allowing them too to bathe in the moonlight. Blue calcite, lapis lazuli, labradorite, selenite, and moonstone are wonderful crystals to channel the Moon's energy.

In the morning, collect the jar and use the moon water in any way you desire! Here are a few ideas:

Cleanse your crystals – Dipping your special crystals in the moon water will refresh and amplify their power.
Aroma mist – Transfer the moon water to a spray bottle and use as a body spray or room mist. You can also add a few drops of your favourite essential oil (optional).
Add to your bath – A bath is a great way to wrangle some of that wild full moon energy! Strain the flowers and add to your bath water, maybe with some epsom salt and a few drops of calming essential oils like lavender.

IN THE KITCHEN

COOKING WITH WATTLESEED

Once the wattle tree has finished flowering, it will develop seed pods. Inside these pods are edible seeds which can be roasted, ground up and turned into a powder, extract, or paste. Wattleseed has a nutty, chocolatey, mild coffee aroma and can be added to breads, beverages or sprinkled over ice cream and desserts. A bush tucker delicacy!

Not all species of wattles produce edible seeds, so I recommend buying it from a reliable source – you will find it in selected wholefood shops, roasted and finely grounded, ready to use.

Health benefits of wattleseed

Wattleseed doesn't only taste delicious, it also has considerable health benefits. A great source of protein, it has a low glycemic index and contains high concentrations of potassium, calcium, iron and zinc.

Here are some recipes that you can try at home.

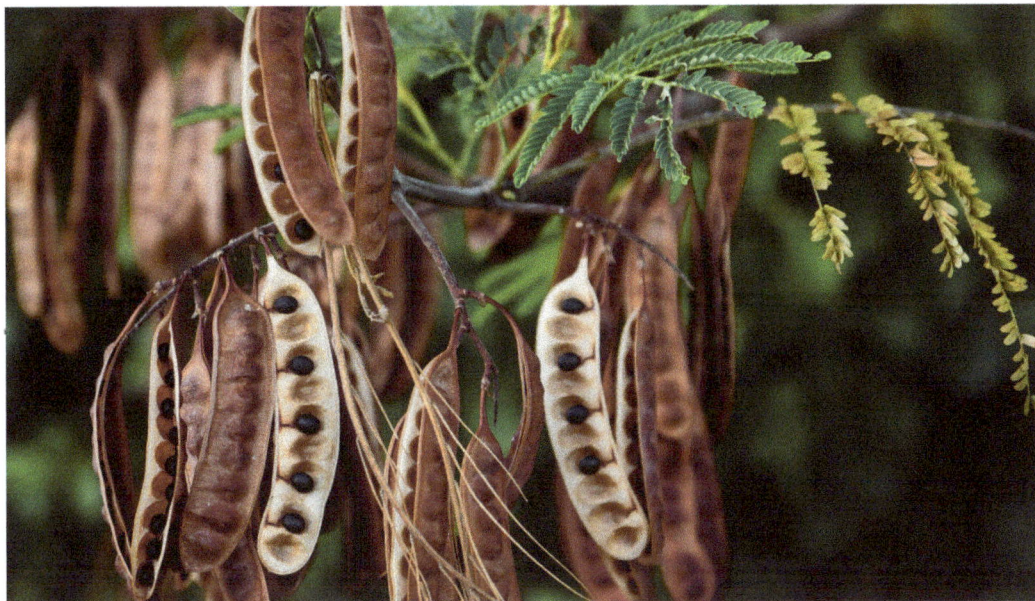

WATTLESEED & MACADAMIA EASY ICE CREAM

A delicious ice cream bursting with Australia's unique native flavours.

Ingredients:

- wattleseed
- macadamias, roughly chopped
- your favourite dairy or plant-based vanilla ice cream

Method. Prepare the wattleseed by measuring out 1 tbsp into a cup and adding 1 tbsp of near-boiling water. Mix and leave to soak for 5 minutes.

Scoop some good quality vanilla ice cream into a bowl and let it soften, then stir through the prepared wattleseed mixture as evenly as possible. Return to the freezer and allow to harden.

Toast the macadamias in a hot, dry pan for a few minutes until just golden. Sprinkle over the ice cream and serve.

WATTLESEED ANZAC BISCUITS

A healthier version of the traditional Anzac biscuits using wholesome, non-refined ingredients.

Ingredients:

- 175g (1 1/2 cups) rolled oats
- 150g (1 1/2 cups) desiccated coconut
- 140g (1 cup) wholemeal spelt flour
- 30g ground wattleseed
- 125ml macadamia nut oil, olive oil or melted butter
- 125ml (1/2 a cup) honey
- 3 tbsp hot water
- 1/2 teaspoon bicarb soda
- 1/2 a cup chopped and toasted macadamias

Method. Preheat the oven to 160°C fan-forced. Combine oats, coconut, spelt flour, wattleseed, macadamia nuts, and bicarb soda into a mixing bowl.

In a separate bowl mix oil, maple syrup, and hot water then add to the dry mix to form a soft dough. Take teaspoonfuls of mixture and place on lightly greased biscuit tray flattening them a little with a fork or with your fingertips. Leave approx. 3cm for the biscuits to spread.

Bake for approx. 20 minutes or until golden. Remove from the oven and cool on wire racks. Enjoy!

"Wattles with your little suns,
underneath the spotted gums,
warm my heart
'till springtime comes,
with your lovely flowers."

NATURE PLAY

PAINTING WATTLES

Introduce your child to pointillism or dot painting. This technique, widely used in Dreamtime art (Aboriginal art based on Dreamtime stories) is easy for little fingers to master and perfect for painting beautiful wattles.

To create the dots you can use a cotton bud or the round eraser tops you find on pencils. These tools will give a lovely three-dimensional effect to the artwork.

We will set up this painting provocation in the Reggio Emilia spirit - read on for more details.

Things to gather:

- paper
- something to make the dots (as listed above)
- earth paint, water based non-toxic paint or coloured stamp pads.

Presenting an activity (a provocation) the Reggio way
In a Reggio-inspired activity items and tools are beautifully arranged and placed in such a way to capture the children's attention, spark wonder, and pique their curiosity. Each item is carefully considered, along with the overall requirements for the activity. Ideally, you don't want to have to scramble to find somewhere for your children to wipe their hands or get more paper while they are painting.

Prepare a designated painting area for each child, with enough paper ready, a drying rack or a predetermined place for their paintings to dry, washcloths for their hands and water and paper towels for the brushes.

Set up the working area with love and purpose. You don't need to have much, but the resources available should be presented in a beautiful and orderly manner.

In this way, we are conveying an important message: That our children's work is valued and respected. As a result, children will likely approach their artwork with the same level of attention and care.

Getting ready to paint

If possible, take a stroll together to pick fresh wattles. Arrange the flowers in a vase or preferably a glass jar, allowing the stems to be visible. Place the jar on top of a flat mirror or mirrored tile, if you have one, to reflect the light and allow for the underside of the flowers to be seen.

Have the paint ready in individual bowls, a paint palette, or a large ice cube tray.

For older children, consider encouraging them to experiment with mixing colours. In addition to yellow paint, you could add some white and brown. Explore the different shades of yellow that can be created.

Let yourself be inspired by the beauty of nature.

NATURE PERFUME

Create your own natural perfume with this favourite sensory play activity. Forage, pinch, sprinkle, mix, grind, and pour – making perfume with real flowers is not only enjoyable, but it also provides an opportunity to explore new words together!

Things to gather:

- wattle and other favourite flowers
- a mortar and pestle
- water
- a strainer
- a small funnel
- spray bottle
- labels (optional)

Directions. Gather some flowers with your child and place them on the play table, along with the mortar and pestle and all the other tools. Mix and grind the flowers, gradually adding water.

Let your concoction sit in the sunshine to allow the flower to release their scent. Then, strain the mixture and carefully pour it into your chosen bottle.

Give your natural perfume a unique name and create a label for your very own signature fragrance.

DYEING WITH WATTLES

Using native plants that are currently in bloom to create natural dyes is a beautiful activity that deepens our connection to the seasons and nature. Rich in tannins, wattles can be used as a dye with or without mordant, producing some beautiful earthy shades.

Things to gather:

- 2 cups wattle flowers
- 1 litre water
- a large stainless-steel saucepan
- soy milk (optional, read note)
- undyed wool yarn, cotton, silk or linen fabric.

Directions. If you want to create colours that are colourfast (meaning they will last forever and won't wash away) you will need to use a mordant to prepare your fabric for dyeing. The function of a mordant is to create a bond between the fibre and the dye. You will find many blogs and books on this topic, and I encourage you to do some research to find what works best for you. For projects with children I love to make a simple soy milk mordant – safe, inexpensive and effective!

STEP 1 - SOY MILK MORDANT

Make a mordant creating a solution of 1 part soy milk to 5 parts water in a deep bucket. Stir well to mix.

Wash your fabric to remove oils, waxes and any other impurities. While still damp, add it to the bucket with the mordant and gently swish it around with tongs or a long wooden spoon. Leave in a cool place to soak for 12-24 hours.

After soaking, use the tongs to remove the fabric and put it in the washing machine for a quick spin cycle. Hang on a clothesline or drying rack to cure for about one week before dyeing.

STEP 2 - PREPARING THE DYE

Add flowers and water to a saucepan. Bring to a boil and let simmer for 20-30 minutes. Take off the heat and let the mixture cool down, then strain the liquid into a clean bowl. Remove the flowers and return the liquid to your saucepan.

Dampen the fabric and add to the saucepan with the dye. Let it simmer on low heat for about 30 minutes, then remove from heat and allow to soak overnight. The longer you soak, the more intense your colour will be.

WATTLE CROWNS

Let the sunshine in with this beautiful winter craft. Using the same technique, you can also make nature crowns and bracelets.

Things to gather:

- strips of cardboard or recycled paper
- double sided sticky tape
- wattle flowers and leaves

Directions. Cut and staple the cardboard to the size required, then attach the wattle flowers using the double-sided sticky tape.

FELT WATTLES

These lovely wattles have been made by wet felting wool roving. Wet felting is great for children. It provides a calming and relaxing sensory experience, all while supporting the development of fine motor skills.

Things to gather:

- wool roving in yellow
- dish soap
- a bowl of hot water
- a bowl of cold clean water
- measuring cups
- towels
- hot glue gun
- florist wire or twigs
- green felt

Prepare your working surface

Cover your working surface with a towel. Add a bowl of warm water (not too hot for the children) and a bowl with cold, clean water.

Make the wattles

To make the wattle blossoms you will need a pillow of wool roving approximately the size of your hand. There is no need to be precise here, but err on the large side as the wool will shrink considerably once you start rolling.

Note: Never cut the length of roving with scissors as this leaves a very blunt end instead of a nice soft edge. Instead, tear the wool with your hands. Hold the wool roving in one hand and pull tufts with the other hand.

Gently open and fluff up the wool fibres so there are no lumps. Rest your pillow of wool in the centre of your hand. With the other hand, squirt one or two drops of dish soap in the middle of the wool and gently spread it around. Now start scrunching up the wool from the centre, then bring your hands around and, very gently, start rolling into a ball. Don't apply too much pressure at this stage.

Dip your ball into hot water whenever it starts to dry out. Keep rolling for about a minute or two, gradually increasing the pressure applied.

You will now begin to see a nice round shape forming, but your ball is likely to be still quite soapy at this stage. Dip it into the cold water and give it a squeeze to release the soap.

Roll again for a few more minutes, until it is firm and dense. Let it dry completely. Repeat the process until you have at least 4 or 5 felted balls. Attach them to various lengths of florist wire (simply poke it with the wire, you can secure it with a drop of hot glue), giving it the appearance of a wattle stem.

Create the leaves

Cut a few rectangles of green felt. Cut the top into a leaf shape but leave the bottom wide and square. This is the area that will glue around the wire to create your leaves.

FIND STEP-BY-STEP VIDEO
INSTRUCTIONS ON HOW TO
MAKE FELT WATTLES ON
OUR WEBSITE

STORYTELLING

THE WATTLE FAIRIES

Have you ever met a Wattle Fairy? These fairies fly so fast, that you might not see them, but only catch the sweet smell of wattle in the air as they flutter by...

Once upon a time there was a happy little girl, so kind and full of joy that everyone called her Sunny. Sunny and her family lived in a small village, where people led a simple life – growing their food, tending the land, raising animals, enjoying the peace of the bush and each other's company.

Sunny's parents worked in a flower farm and Sunny always thought she was the luckiest girl in the world. She loved flowers. She loved their colours, their smell, the different shapes and how every morning there seem to be new buds opening to the sun.

Every day Sunny would pick a bundle of flowers for her mama, which she would place on the kitchen table, one for her herself, to keep in her bedroom, and another small one to place in her fairy garden. Sunny hoped the fairies would love her gift and that one day, they would allow her to see them.

But one early winter afternoon, a dry wind swept across the village bringing dust and fire. That night, glowing orange flames burnt trees, and plants and all the vegetables and all the flowers growing.

People were left with very little. Their homes were empty, their gardens were bare. The streets looked grim, black and burnt... all the colours seemed to have been washed away. Everyone in the village tried to be brave, but nobody could be their usual, cheerful self.

Even Sunny felt sad. She missed the colours and she really hoped there was something she could do to bring them back.

And then, one morning Sunny woke up to something unexpected. Overnight, just like magic, the wattle trees outside her home had bloomed. Their branches were now full of yellow flowers — round and bright like little suns.

"How beautiful these wattles are" said Sunny. She closed her eyes and inhaled deeply. Oh, how she had missed the colour and the smell of flowers.

Suddenly, she heard a voice. It was gentle and sweet like music and soft as a breeze, but Sunny could hear the words clearly, as if they were whispered in her ear.

"Sunny the kindest we've come to greet. Garlands of wattle we lay at your feet. Joyful and happy may you always be. Bright as the blessings of the wattle tree!"

Sunny looked around in astonishment. The Wattle Fairies were singing to her! There they were... yellow, fluffy-haired, round-eyed and so, so beautiful.

"Why are you sad, sweet child?" they asked her.
"The fires have taken away the colours of the flowers and the smiles of people. I wish I could do something to help," said Sunny.

"Dear Sunny, always so kind and caring. Take this gift of love gathered with our own hands and stored in our blossoms. It will bring people joy and happiness. It will remind them that spring is not far. The Sun will shine again, and the Earth will grow bountiful and colourful once more. Hold out your apron now, Sunny and catch it".

The fairies flew to the tree and gently shook the branches. Down came a shower of pure gold... hundreds of wattle flowers, light and fluffy and so fragrant. Sunny's little apron was heavy, but she held on tightly so not even one would fall.

Quickly, she ran to the village and gave each person a sprig of wattle flowers. People hurried inside their houses to grab glasses and jars filled with water to keep their special gift. Their homes were now glowing with golden light. Everyone was smiling again. Like the first ray of sunshine after a cold night, the wattles had filled their hearts with warmth and hope.

"How can I ever thank you, dear Wattle Fairies?" Sunny went back to the wattle tree, the very first one to bloom, searching for them.

But as fairies always do, they had vanished as suddenly as they had come, leaving behind only a sprinkle of magic, and the sweet scent of spring.

SEPTEMBER

GENTLE WHISPERINGS OF LIFE STIRRING

"The last thunderstorm in autumn told the animals to go to sleep, and the first big clap of thunder in early spring woke them up again and brought them out of hibernation." – Charles Moran, Bundjalung Elder[6]

Spring... the season of birds nesting and singing, of flowers blooming, of early sunny mornings warm enough for us to want to kick off our shoes and feel the damp earth under our bare feet. In the air, there's a tangible sense of excitement — a delicate yet fierce promise of life returning. Can you feel it, too?

Spring offers an invitation to be present — a celebration of the myriad of marvels that come alive as soon as we become just a little more attentive, a little more open.

While our calendars mark the first day of spring on September 1, we are learning to read the seasons by observing the natural world — seeing, feeling, experiencing. There's something profoundly enchanting about witnessing these transitions. Nature is always changing, still each time feels like an entirely new story unfolding before our eyes.

What big and little joys will this season bring forth? All around us, Mother Earth is stirring. We witness spring's arrival in the trees, the plants, and the animals. What is changing in the world around you? Look attentively and see if you can detect these signs of spring.

SIGNS OF SPRING

NESTING BIRDS

Spring signals the start of nesting season for many birds. During this time, which generally runs over six to eight weeks, parent birds will be extra protective of their nest and hatchlings.

Here in Australia, magpies are amongst the most noticeable nesters. Watch them collect sticks, grasses, and pet fur, and carry them to their tree in preparation for the arrival of their precious offspring! During the six weeks when their chicks are fledgling – meaning they are growing feathers and learning to fly – mama and papa magpies are on high alert. They fiercely guard their nest from any perceived threats, and this protective behaviour is known as swooping.

Meanwhile, kookaburras are busy searching for hollows and termite mounds in trees to use as their nests. You might even witness some squabbles as they compete for prime nesting sites! In September, they will lay their first clutch of eggs, and towards the end of spring, their adorable, fluffy chicks will emerge, joyfully practising their signature laugh as they take flight.

BIRDSONG

The best time to hear birds sing is at dawn on a spring morning. As the Sun rises, birds excitedly welcome the new day with a symphony, creating one of nature's most magnificent musical displays. Well worth getting up early for!

Some young birds learn to sing in spring. During the early stages of their learning, they often just babble, much like human babies do. They listen to adults of their own species sing and with practice and patience they learn to imitate them, often adding their own little special touch.

FLOWERING TREES AND WILDFLOWERS

Wattles are now blooming across parks, gardens and roadsides. While some varieties have been covered in fluffy yellow blossoms since August, the majority of wattle trees will continue to flower throughout September.

Silky oaks (*Grevillea robusta*) paint the sky and our streets with luscious brush strokes of warm yellow and orange. With flowers literally dripping with nectar, they are feeding, nesting and roosting havens for small native birds as well as bees.

In our national parks, native orchids and other wildflowers are beginning to make their appearance. Heath flowers (usually growing along exposed coastal or mountain ridges) are blooming everywhere – a clear indication that spring has unmistakably arrived.

How many wildflowers can you spot, and where are they growing? Capture their beauty in your nature journal through sketches and observations. Take time to research which native flower represents your state, and why, and see if you can find it growing in the wild.

AWAKENING FROM SLEEP

Many creatures are now ready to awaken from their winter slumber. Microbats stir as the weather warms, while large bats like grey-headed flying foxes become more active due to the abundance of their favourite fruits and flowers.

Lizards, skinks, geckos, dragons, and snakes emerge from their winter torpor and venture out in search of warmth.

Spring is the most likely time of the year to encounter snakes, basking in the sun on rocks or footpaths. Ensure that everyone in your family, including children, knows and practises safe behaviour around snakes.

HUMPBACK WHALES

Humpback whales are migrating south, to return to their home in Antarctica, swimming closer to our shores to keep their young safe. This is an exciting time as we can spot mama whales travelling with their newborn calves!

BABY STEPS

Baby koalas, called joeys (just like baby kangaroos), are typically born in January or February, and by spring they are ready to venture out of the pouch for the first time.

At this stage, joeys are still very small and cling to their mother's belly while nursing regularly. But later in the season, as they grow bigger and more curious, they will ride on their mother's back. Look up the tall gumtrees in your area to spot them!

In eastern and southern Australia, koala mating occurs between September and March. Listen out for the bellowing sounds of male koalas looking to mate. Their grunts and bellows are so loud they can sometimes be heard several kilometres away!

Bear in mind that koalas are frequently down on the ground at this time of year, moving between trees in their search for mates and territory. Remember to drive slowly around your neighbourhood!

BECOME A WILDLIFE RESCUER

You are walking along your street or playing at the park when you hear a loud chirping. A baby bird is on the ground, looking lost and abandoned.
What can you do to help?

NOT FOR ADOPTION

Birds are often knocked out of nests during high winds, storms and even when learning to fly. If you find a baby bird on the ground, resist the temptation of taking it. It's not up for adoption! Its parents are most likely nearby, and despite our love and best intentions, they can take better care of it than we do. Instead, follow these steps to become a knowledgeable wildlife rescuer.

First, determine if the bird actually needs help. Is it a nestling or a fledgling? Here's how you can tell the difference.

Nestlings have few or no feathers, and if found on the ground, they certainly need your help. These baby birds are still unable to fly and are too young to leave the nest.

Fledglings are fully feathered juvenile birds who are learning to fly. They still have a very short tail and short wing feathers. You may come across them hopping along on the ground, perching on low-hanging branches, or hiding under bushes.
Like you, they are exploring! If they're not injured and look healthy, just let them be.

If it's a healthy nestling you found on the ground, the first thing you want to do is locate the nest and place the bird back in it quickly. If you can't see or reach the nest, or if you can see that it has been destroyed, create a temporary home using a hanging basket, kitchen strainer, or a small plastic container (like an empty ice cream tub) with holes punched in the bottom.

Ideally the "nest" should be cereal-bowl shaped, well padded with tissue paper, bracken, grass or leaves. Use non-slippery material, or the bird's legs could spread out sideways and become deformed. Fasten the nest in a sheltered area to the bird's original location, ensuring that it's out of reach of any cats or dogs.

Almost always the parents will return to care for their baby. Watch quietly from a distance. In the unlikely event that the parents don't return to feed the nestling, follow the steps below for helping an orphaned baby bird.

HOW TO HELP AN ORPHANED OR INJURED BIRD

If, after several hours, the parents have not returned, or if the nestling or fledgling is either ill or injured, this is what you can do.

Create a safe home – Line a cardboard box or plastic container with a paper towel and place the bird in it (make sure you have clean hands and use gloves or a towel). Make sure the baby bird's legs are tucked underneath its body, not stretched out.

Keep the bird warm and quiet – You can do this by covering it with a paper towel or placing a small hot water bottle inside the box (but not touching the bird). Place your temporary nest in a warm, quiet and dark, away from pets. Noise can be very stressful for baby birds and they are likely to be very scared, so limit your contact with it and be as quiet as possible around it.

Do not offer the baby bird any food or water – It can be tempting to show our love and care by offering food. It is important to remember however that every species requires a specific diet and we can make the bird more ill or weak by giving it food it should not eat.

Get help – Do not keep the baby bird or try to treat it yourself. Instead, contact your local wildlife centre and arrange to take the bird to a place where experienced rehabilitators can take care of it.

EARTH MAGIC

AUSTRALIAN MAGPIES

Have you ever been woken up by the morning song of magpies? Their melodic carolling is a familiar sound of the Australian landscape, and one of the most complex birdsong in the world.

Aboriginal Dreamtime stories tell us that it is the boastful song of the magpie that each morning raises the sky from the Earth to bring us a new day. However, magpies are not only amazing singers. Playful, social and protective, they are extremely intelligent birds. Let's get to know them a bit better!

- Magpies occupy the same territory for their entire life. Once they find a suitable home, they will stay there for up to 20-25 years.

- Magpies are clever mimics. They can imitate other birds' calls, dogs barking and even say human words.

- Magpies have phenomenal hearing – they can hear the sound of grubs and worms under the ground. If you see a magpie turn its head to the side while walking across the grass, it's probably zeroing in on the location of its next meal.

- They recognise people. Magpies have an exceptional visual memory. They can remember and recognise up to 100 human faces and they will treat people differently depending on whether they think they are friends or a threat.

- Female magpies build their own nests from sticks and then line them with wool, pet hair, grass and string to keep their eggs warm and toasty. Eggs are blueish-green with brown spots.

- For most of the year they follow us around, loyal companions of our backyards. But during nesting season some magpies can become fiercely protective and swoop people and smaller animals who come too close – often inadvertently – to their nests. This behaviour only lasts for a short period of time, and it's typical of males.

So, don't mess with a magpie or you will most likely get swooped. But be kind to the magpies in your neighbourhood, and they will be kind to you. Help them when they're in need, keep your dog away from them and occasionally slip them some food. Sunflower seeds are a favourite treat!

A POEM FOR MAMA MAGPIE

Her plumage is black with splashes of white
Searching the ground a magpie's in sight,
Her eyes are bright, like golden sun
She greets the day when morning's begun.

She fluffs up her feathers, sings her sweet song
Guarding her ground all day long.

When spring arrives, she starts her quest
to build a cosy but messy nest
High up a tree, alert and brave
She keeps her eggs warm and safe.

And meanwhile we wonder, watching with glee
How many chicks will soon come to be?"

WHAT'S IN A SONG?

Magpies begin to produce sounds soon after they are born, and the complexity of their songs develops as they grow. They may make high pitched calls to signal danger or distress, or to request food. But magpies are mostly recognised for their warbling, duetting and carolling. Listen carefully to spot the difference.

Warbling
A magpie in solitude will emit a quiet, melodic warble. It is the delightful sound we often hear throughout the day and sometimes at night. Warbling has no specific purpose – it is just the magpie enjoying and singing to life.

Duetting
Duetting is a conversation in song – one magpie sings and another responds. It is used to determine the location of group members and may also identify them.

Carolling
Groups of magpies will burst into a loud song to proclaim their territory. This is called carolling. There is usually one bird leading and others joining in to sing the same song.

High pitch calls
The babies and young ones emit continuous high-pitched short noises when hungry – they are begging for food! Adult magpies also use a series of high-pitched sounds when threatened or in distress. It's an alarm call for danger.

Moonlight song
Australian magpies sometimes sing at night, a beautiful melody of repetitive phrases often referred to as a moonlight song.

FULL MOON

MOON BREATHING

A simple grounding pranayama practice to help quiet your mind and calm your body. Peaceful dreams guaranteed!

Moon breathing is an ancient practice known by yogis as **chandra bhedana**. This breathing technique channels the cooling energy of the Moon, helping us relax and ground the mind and the body. In Sanskrit, chandra is the name for moon and bhedana means 'passing through'.

You can use this breath with your little ones when they need some quiet time, to restore calm, and to prepare for a restful night's sleep. Here is how we practise it.

- Sit in a comfortable upright position. Take a few rounds of full, deep belly breaths – imagine your belly creating the shape of a full moon.

- Using your right thumb close the right nostril and take a slow, deep inhale through the left nostril.

- Hold the breath for as long as comfortable.

- Block the left nostril and exhale through the right nostril.

- This is one round of chandra bhedana pranayama. Continue for 5 to 10 rounds, repeating the same process.

- To finish, take a slow deep breath through both nostrils, and relax into your natural breath.

IN THE KITCHEN

CREATE A SPRING CLEANSING RITUAL

Springtime brings a glorious awakening not only in nature but also in our body. As the land flourishes, we, too, feel ready to shake off the dreariness of winter.

Creating practices and rituals that allow us to live in alignment with the seasons can support our physical, emotional and spiritual wellbeing – balancing the immune system, digestive pathways, and helping us restore vitality and harmony within ourselves.

Spring cleansing is a beautiful practice that can help us connect to the emerging and clearing energy of this season.

WHAT IS SPRING CLEANSING?

A spring cleanse is a self-care ritual that harnesses the nourishing and detoxifying properties of spring greens – the first wild herbs to emerge in this season – to restore and renew our body, mind and energy levels.

These plants, often referred to as 'spring tonics', are vibrating with life force energy. There are nasturtiums, nettles, dandelion leaves, cleavers, and violets, just to name a few. Look around you and you will most likely find a bouquet of spring blooms brimming with medicinal benefits. Simply incorporate them into your meals or set some nourishing self-care time apart to make our delicious Spring Elixir.

SPRING TONICS

Look at what is growing in your garden or in your neighbourhood but make sure that you can identify the plants with certainty. If in doubt, check with your local naturopath or herbalist. The plants listed below are edible and generally considered safe for healthy adults.

Nettle
Hailed as the ultimate spring tonic, nettle is a refreshing and delicious wild green known for its cleansing and blood building properties. It is also one of nature's most nutrient-dense plants, being an exceptional source of iron, calcium, magnesium, silica and potassium.

Harvest nettle with a pair of scissors and tongs or use rubber gloves to avoid stinging. Young tips are less fibrous and most flavourful.

Dandelion
Both the root and leaves of dandelions are packed with therapeutic benefits and have a long history of use in traditional medicine as a digestive aid and liver tonic among other things.

Dandelion greens have a bitter flavour, which is attenuated when cooked. The yellow flower petals can also be eaten – add them raw to your salad or cooked in baked goodies.

Violet
Both the leaves and flowers of the common blue violet are edible and medicinal. The leaves are high in vitamins A and C, and contain a good bit of mucilage, a soluble fibre helpful in lowering cholesterol levels and supporting gut health. Violet roots aren't edible, so remove them prior to using.

Cooked or raw, these greens are delicious and packed with nutrients and can be added practically to any meal – from smoothies to salads to ice cream and cakes.

Another option is to enjoy them as herbal tea – simply harvest the leaves or flower petals, rinse and steep for at least 15 minutes in boiling water and strain. Or leave them in the water overnight and enjoy the next day as a nourishing cold tonic.

SPRING ELIXIR

I love making Spring Elixir. The recipe below is inspired by the amazing herbalist and author Erin Lovell Verinder, and it's fail-proof! Just use whatever is in bloom and bountiful around you.

Ingredients:

- a mix of spring greens and flowers, rinsed and dried
- raw apple cider vinegar

Method. Add your greens and flowers to a sterilised mason jar – you want your jar to be around 3/4 full with plant material.

Fill with vinegar ensuring the herbs are completely covered. Seal the jar with a plastic lid (metal might create corrosion). Shake well and store for 4-6 weeks. When the elixir is ready, strain and decant into a sterilised glass bottle.

Enjoy as a salad dressing, drizzled over veggies, add to sparkling water for a delicious shrub, or take it neat off a spoon!

NATURE PLAY

BUILD A NEST

When spring arrives, we can help our bird friends by offering nesting material. Collect natural, biodegradable, pesticide-free nesting materials such as scraps of coloured yarn and wool roving, dry grass and fallen leaves, twigs and strips of bark.

Tuck your nesting material in the crook of a tree or in a shrub where you've noticed bird activity (even better if sheltered from the rain). Get your adventure binoculars out and keep an eye for colourful nests in the trees around you.

Extensions
What do birds use to build their nests? How do they make them? And how do they choose the best spot for them? Search your backyard for twigs, dried grass, leaves and bark and **try to arrange them into a nest shape**.
Gather soft and light materials and fill in the inside of the nest. It's not that easy, right? Yet birds can create these wonderful homes just out of simple resources they find in nature, and they do it without hands!

Make some eggs with playdough or by rolling mud into ball shapes.

Do you think we could make **a nest big enough for us**? Build a nest out of blankets, scarves, pillows and other objects you have available. Turn it into a quiet area where you can get cosy and read a book together.

Play bird! Once the nest is complete, children can have fun playing mother bird sitting on the eggs or they can be the baby birds, chirping for their snack. Follow the children's lead and let the play take flight!

THE SECRET LANGUAGE OF BIRDS

Birds are the secret messengers of the forest – learn to interpret their language!

Birds love to chatter about what's going on around them at all times. They don't simply sit on a branch and sing – they communicate with each other using different sounds and calls, depending on what they are doing and experiencing.

Birds are always vigilant. They know everything that is happening in the forest, because their life depends on it. By listening to the birds and understanding their language you can tell if an animal is nearby, maybe a predator, or if another person is walking along the trail – just from the way they are chirping.

So how do you learn bird language?

Magpies, kookaburras, rainbow lorikeets, noisy miners, willy wagtails and honeyeaters are some of our most recognisable backyard birds. Choose one that comes to visit you often. Use your binoculars to observe the bird and have something handy to note your observations – your nature journal, a smartphone or any other recording device (optional).

Bird language can be sorted into five categories:

- **Song** – A bird's signature sound
- **Companion call** – The sounds birds use to talk with each other during feeding or travel
- **Juvenile begging** – The high pitch noises chicks and young birds make to get adults to feed them. They are saying "I'm hungry!"
- **Aggression** – The sounds made by birds defending their territory against other intruding birds
- **Alarm call** – There is a threat!

Can you identify these songs and calls?

BIRD SHAPES

Making birds out of clay or playdough is a favourite activity for many children. You can shape the birds with your hands or use a cookie cutter. Once dry, you can paint them and maybe even add some real feathers! Draw inspiration from books or images, or maybe from the birds you have encountered in your backyard.

Playdough is a great option for younger children - use our fail-proof recipe below to make some together.

Things to gather:

- 1 cup organic all-purpose wheat flour
- 200ml water
- 2 tsp cream of tartar
- 2 tbsp salt
- 1 tbsp vegetable oil
- earth pigments or food colours (optional)

Directions. In a small pot, mix water with a pinch of earth pigments or a few drops of food colour, if using. Add salt and cream of tartar and warm it up until dissolved.

Place the flour into a large bowl and add about half of the water mix. Stir with a wooden spoon, gradually adding more water (you can always add a bit more if needed, or more flour if you use too much water). Start kneading it with your hands into a smooth dough.

Make an indentation in the dough and pour the vegetable oil in it. Knead for a few more seconds, until the oil is thoroughly mixed in.

Place the dough into a plastic bag and leave it for 15-30 minutes. This step really helps make it silky and smooth. Knead it a bit more, and it's ready to play with!

STORYTELLING

A NEST FOR MAMA MAGPIE

Once upon a time, a long time ago, all the birds were busy learning bird things. They learnt how to fly and what to eat. They learnt how to sing. They learnt to build nests to keep their chicks safe and warm.

But the beautiful Australian magpie, with her striking black and white feathers, didn't get any further than the singing. She sang joyfully all day long, carolling, chortling, and whistling away.

"Listen to me, just listen to my beautiful voice," she would say. Magpie sang to the Moon and to the rising Sun, happy as any bird could be.

Springtime arrived and all the birds were building nests. Everyone except the magpie, of course. Suddenly she realised that she had no idea how to build one!

"Please tell me," she pleaded, "tell me how to build my nest."

The other birds felt sorry for the poor magpie, and so they decided to help her out. Early in the morning, a crowd of them gathered around. Each one of them had brought something from their own nest to share with the magpie – there were sticks and twigs, mud, and bark, grass and cobwebs.

"Poof! Who needs any of that stuff?" the kookaburra laughed. "Just find a hollow in a tree, as cockatoo and I do. It's the best place to bring up a family."

"A hollow tree is no place to build a nest," jumped in the noisy miner. "Build your nest in the tree canopy, amongst the soft leaves. Find the strongest branch and make it yours."

"Yes, yes, the tree canopy is good, but make sure it's well hidden. You want your nest to blend in and camouflage. Use small sticks and only the softest grass – spider webs will keep them together. Oh, oh and a bit of bark on the outside as a final touch!" squeaked the willy wagtail.

"Not sticks, not grass!" shrieked the welcome swallow. "Build in mud, wet mud, under a rock or branch. Your nest must be perfectly round. That's the nest for you, magpie."

"Nooo way! The best nest is on the ground," announced the brush turkey. "Make a biiiig mound with leaves and soil, like I do. It's soft and so, soooo warm."

"Who even needs to build a nest? I don't bother at all!" announced the channel-billed cuckoo. "I let other birds do all the hard work and then I lay my eggs inside their nests."

"Build a nest you are proud of! Make it large and heavy, and place it in the tallest tree so you can get a good view of your territory," said the wedge-tailed eagle.

Poor Mama magpie was feeling rather tired. She was even more confused than before!

"Now, just listen to me," hooted the wise barking owl. "We are different birds and we build different nests. You will find your own. But whatever you do, what is truly important is that you always protect it. Keep it safe, no matter what."

"Yes," decided the magpie, "that's what I shall do."

And so in no time, she found a tall gumtree and started working on her nest. She threw together some sticks and twigs. She added some hair, feathers and wool that she had found. A bit of wire went in there, too. It wasn't the prettiest of nests. It wasn't tidy, nor soft, not particularly big nor particularly small. But Mama magpie thought it was just fine, and she laid four spotted eggs inside it.

She sat on them. The wind blew and the rain came, but she did not move. She let no bird or creature come close to her precious nest. Three weeks later, that messy nest was home to four squawking, hungry little magpies. Mama magpie taught them how to fly. She taught them to search for food. She taught them how to sing as beautifully as she did — but she could not teach them how to build a tidy nest.

And so to this very day, Australian magpies build nests that are messy, and unruly. But you know what? They really don't mind.
They'd rather spend their time singing!

A mama magpie collecting
materials for her nest

OCTOBER

FIND YOUR WINGS

Rainbow lorikeets sing joyfully to the sweet honeysuckles in bloom. Insects of all kinds – bees, wasps, butterflies – emerge from their hidden retreats. Streets are covered with delicate purple petals – it's time for the jacarandas to put on their grand display.

The essence of spring is one of both fragility and strength. The air feels light and crisp, gentle breezes carrying the promise of warmer weather. But it is also a season of determination, as nature triumphs over the cold grasp of winter, signalling a time of growth and rejuvenation. Tender buds, colourful wildflowers, delicate seedlings. Life bursting forth from every corner.

October can be moody and capricious – a sunny day can quickly give way to a sudden downpour, chilly mornings shift into hot afternoons. We learn to adapt and embrace its unpredictability – packing layers of extra clothes and keeping raincoats and gumboots always handy!

EARTH MAGIC

BUTTERFLY MIGRATION

Imagine standing on a beach, on a crisp sunny morning when suddenly the sky is filled with joyful fluttering – thousands of butterflies are dancing around you! It's not a dream. You are witnessing a butterfly migration – one of those moments when we come face to face with the magic of nature.

What is happening?

Certain groups of butterflies are known to migrate in large masses – flying long distances, gracefully moving together towards a purposeful destination. They might need to find a breeding site where there is an abundance of plants on which they can lay their eggs, or a warm, sheltered location where they can cluster together over the cold winter months.

Two species of butterflies that migrate in such spectacular ways here in Australia are the caper white butterfly and the blue tiger butterfly. Let's learn a little more about them.

CAPER WHITE BUTTERFLY (BELENOIS JAVA)

Caper whites are beautiful white butterflies with yellow and black markings. In spring these butterflies embark on a strenuous journey of over 3,000kms, flying throughout South Australia, New South Wales and Queensland to areas where caper bushes are abundant. These are the plants on which they will lay their eggs and will feed their larvae.

If you happen to find these butterflies on your garden plants or in your veggie patch, they are most likely there to rest before continuing their flight.

They need a lot of energy to make it to their destination and we can help them by offering some sweet, delicious treats – find the recipes in this month's Nature Play section.

A migration of caper white butterflies is a natural phenomenon which happens on an irregular basis. Sometimes it's an annual occurrence; other times it can be years apart.

Enjoy this beautiful sight as it happens.

BLUE TIGER BUTTERFLY (TIRUMALA HAMATA)

Blue tiger butterflies are large dark brown or black butterflies, with light blue markings dotted across their wings.

During spring and summer, these butterflies move en masse towards southern Queensland, New South Wales, and even Victoria. But in autumn, they return to the coastal rainforests of northern Queensland, where they wait out the cooler months huddled together on trees and vines in sheltered gullies and creek banks.

The blue tigers are one of the longest living butterfly species, living up to six months. Considering that some other species only live for two weeks, that is quite a lifespan!

Their longevity might have something to do with their diet, which consists mainly of… poisonous plants! Blue tiger caterpillars love to munch on the leaves of the Corky Milk vine, a toxic plant. Not only the caterpillars are immune to the poison, but once ingested, the toxic chemicals of this plant work as protection for the adult butterfly.

Our native birds have learnt that they get sick from eating blue tigers, and so they wisely leave them alone. How incredible!

CAPER WHITE BUTTERFLY

BLUE TIGER BUTTERFLY

FULL MOON

FOLLOW THE JOURNEY OF THE MOON WITH A PHENOLOGY WHEEL

As the year unfolds, we have been gradually, but consistently, working on honing our observation skills. Most of the time, we find ourselves observing passively, inadvertently missing out on the richness of life that surrounds us. The art of true observation requires conscious effort to improve it, much like training a muscle to function better.

Over the last few months, we have been observing and honouring the full moon — a time of radiant light and expansion. But what about the other moon phases?

Understanding the lunar cycle is a fascinating process, with each phase bringing different energy and opening up our awareness to how vast, complex, and perfect our Universe is.

UNDERSTANDING LUNAR PHASES

The Moon orbits the Earth, constantly circling around our planet. It takes the moon approximately 29.5 days to complete a full circle, which is known as a lunar month. During this time, the moon goes through various phases, as depicted in the image below.

If we could magically look at the solar system from above, we would notice that half of the Moon is always illuminated by the Sun, while the other half remains in darkness. As the Moon orbits the Earth, the portion of the lit side that we see changes, leading to different phases. These phases repeat in the same order over and over again.

When the Moon is positioned between the Earth and the Sun, the side that we see is in total darkness. This is called a **new moon** phase.

But as it moves away from the Sun, a thin sliver of the Moon becomes visible in the sky, growing larger each night.

When half of the Moon is illuminated, we call it the **first quarter moon**, signifying that the Moon is one-quarter of the way through the lunar month (even though we see half of it). The Moon continues to wax (grow larger) until it reaches the **full moon** phase, when we can see its entire sunlit face.

The full moon rises almost exactly as the Sun sets and sets just as the Sun rises the next day. At this stage, the Moon has completed one half of its journey around the Earth.

During the second half of the lunar month, the Moon starts to wane (grow thinner) each night. When it reaches the third quarter point, we once again see one side of its disc illuminated and the other side in darkness, but the sides have now swapped over.

Finally, the Moon completes its journey and transitions back to the new moon phase, and a new cycle begins. The illustration below shows the side of the Moon that is lit by the Sun and the corresponding lunar phase we see from Earth.

THE MOON AS SEEN FROM EARTH [7]

We, as human beings, are also cyclical beings, and whether we are conscious of it or not, the moon's monthly cycle can have an impact on our lives.

We may feel its tugs and movements, affecting our mood and state of mind. Observing the moon can provide us with a quiet space, both around and within us, where we can set our intentions.

To facilitate our observations, this month we will create a moon phenology wheel. Phenology wheels are used to depict and keep track of what's happening in nature during a certain period of time.

Using the template here included you can record daily moon phases – a wonderful excuse to bundle up and get outside for a few minutes to marvel at the night sky.

Photocopy the following pages or download them as a free resource from our website (scan the QR code on page 14).

Curiosity
For those of us living in the Southern Hemisphere, the Moon appears 'upside down' compared to the Northern Hemisphere. This means that the side which is shining (sunlit) appears to be the opposite from what those in the Northern Hemisphere observe.

PHASES OF THE MOON

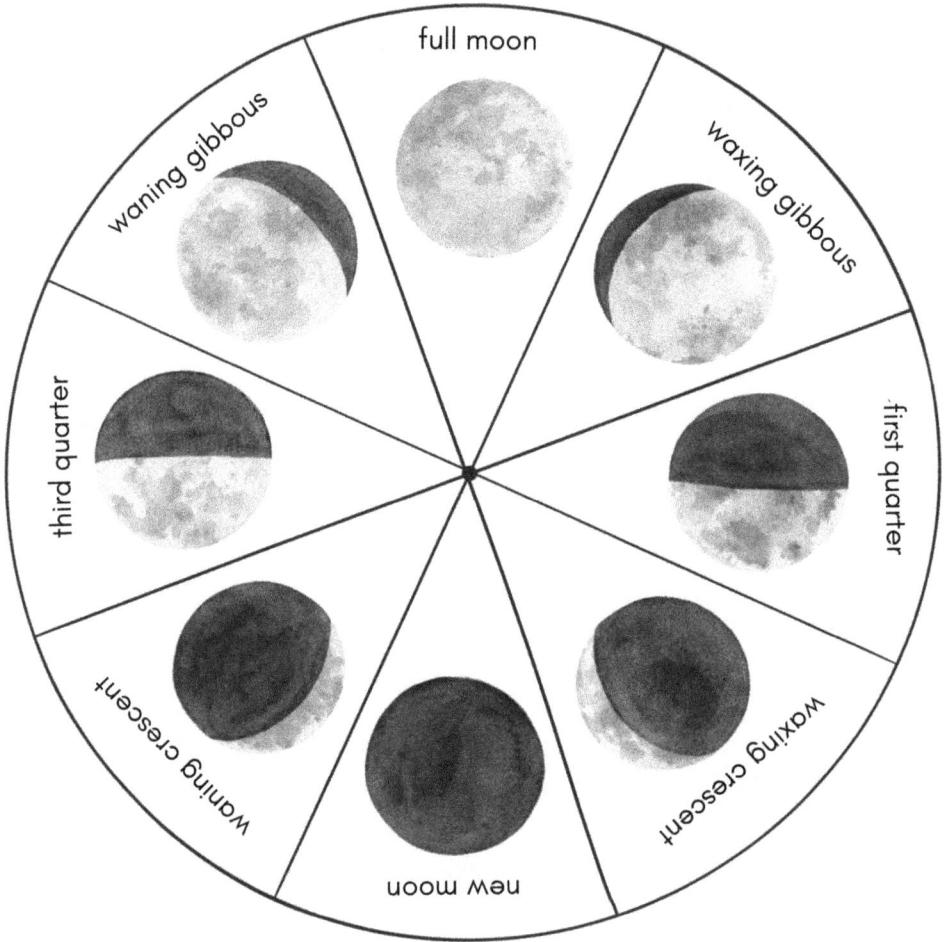

full moon

waxing gibbous

waning gibbous

first quarter

third quarter

waxing crescent

waning crescent

new moon

LUNAR STUDY
MONTH: _____

IN THE KITCHEN

SPRING PICNIC

Lovely spring sunny days provide the perfect setting for picnics in nature. We cherish simplicity – sometimes all you need is a loaf of freshly baked bread and some butter. Delicious comfort food that soothes the heart and satisfies hungry bellies!

This month, we'll learn how to make both fresh bread and butter, and our children will be our eager little helpers, of course. So, let's get those aprons ready and create some homemade goodness together.

FRESH BUTTER IN A JAR

I love creamy, smooth, and mouth-melting butter spread on a warm slice of bread. Pure, simple, and uncomplicated goodness.

Making butter at home is actually really easy, and fun. All it takes is good quality cream, water, salt, a mason jar... and lots of energy to jump, shake and dance. Do you know anyone in your house who might have some?

Seriously, making fresh butter is one of the easiest and most satisfying homestead activities that you will ever do. The process is so straightforward that children are likely to complete it from start to finish with minimal assistance.

Ingredients:

- pure cream (organic, if possible)
- a mason jar
- a colander
- baking paper
- two marbles (optional)
- salt, herbs, edible flowers (optional)

Method. Start by placing two clean marbles in the jar. While the marbles aren't essential, they add a fun element to the process. If you don't have them handy, feel free to skip this step.

Next, fill the jar with cream, but not more than halfway full, and seal the lid tightly. Ensure that the lid is properly closed, or you might end up covered in cream!

Now, the fun part begins – shake vigorously. Shake up and down, shake with your whole body, shake and jump, shake and dance, shake to music and shake to silly songs you make up as you go. This is a great energy release!

Pass the jar around and let children and adults take turns. This butter is made with love and joyous vibrations.

Initially, the marbles will clank as they shake with the cream, but as the liquid thickens, you won't hear the sound anymore. This indicates that the cream is transforming into butter. Take a peek inside to see how it's changing.

We are not done yet... keep shaking a little more. Soon you will hear the unmistakable 'clank, clank' of the marbles again as they hit against the side of the jar. Now, the cream has fully separated. Congratulations, you've just made butter!

Open the jar – you will see a cluster of yellow butter surrounded by liquid buttermilk. Transfer the buttermilk in a separate container and set aside for later use. Remove the marbles.

Rinse the butter under cold water, gently massaging it with your hands to squeeze all the remaining liquid out of it. At this point, you can add a pinch of salt, chopped herbs like rosemary and thyme, or even edible flowers if you want.

With the palm of your hands, gently roll the butter into a small piece of baking paper, creating a lovely log shape. If you can resist the temptation of devouring it all at once, store it in the fridge.

Blessings and magic.

Children enjoy making fresh butter during our forest school program

HONEY WHEAT BREAD ROLLS

When both my children were little, we attended a beautiful Waldorf playgroup. Among the many activities, making bread rolls was their absolute favourite. There was something magical about kneading the dough, shaping it with our hands, and savouring the warm rolls as morning tea before heading home.

So when I started our nature playgroups, I knew I wanted to carry on this heartwarming tradition. Before diving into playtime, we gather around a big table, where we knead, sing, and shape the dough together. Once the rolls are baked to perfection, we sit under a big gum tree, and enjoy them warm with honey and cinnamon. It's a moment of pure joy and connection.

Over time, I have tried and tested many recipes, but this remains my favourite and a very easy one to follow.

Ingredients:

- 2 tbsp dry yeast
- 3 cups warm liquid
- 1/4 cup plus 1 tbsp honey
- 1/3 cup olive oil or melted butter
- 3 tsp salt
- 6-8 cups of flour mixture (wheat, white – 2 cups of the mixture can be oatmeal which gives a nice texture, millet, seeds, etc)

Method. Mix yeast, 1 tbsp of honey and some warm water in a bowl. Allow the mixture to foam up. In a separate large bowl, combine warm liquid, oil, honey, and the foamed yeast mixture. Add the sifted flour, and the salt as the last ingredient. Stir until the liquid is fully absorbed.

As we stir, we sing:

"The farmer gave us golden grain for us to grind and grind. Now it's flour brown and white, soft and very fine. Add the water, yeast and honey, mix it with our hands. When it's soft and not too runny we will let it stand."

Let the mixture stand for 5 minutes, then begin kneading the dough. Gradually add more flour during kneading until the dough becomes smooth and elastic. Cover the dough and let it rise for one hour.

Shape the dough into small rolls and place them on an oiled baking sheet.

In a bowl, add a splash of milk (of any type). Using a kitchen brush, "paint" the bread rolls with the milk. This will give them a nice golden top. If time allows, let the rolls rest for another 15 minutes before baking.

Bake at 180C for 20 minutes or until golden brown. Let it cool slightly before serving with fresh butter and a drizzle of honey.

Best enjoyed outside!

NOTES

Warm liquid: Your liquid can be water or milk, or a combination of both to make 3 cups. You can also add the buttermilk collected from the butter! Heat in the microwave for 30 seconds or gently warm on the stovetop.

Flour: Start with 6 cups, and gradually add more to achieve a smooth, elastic dough that is not too sticky. I use 4 cups of good quality stone ground white flour and 2 cups wholemeal flour or oatmeal, but you can experiment with your own blend.

NATURE PLAY

MAKE A BUTTERFLY FEEDER

Butterflies are not only beautiful but also serve as essential pollinators that play a crucial role in helping our trees and plants thrive. With their notable sweet tooth, attracting butterflies to your garden is a breeze! Let's begin by preparing some sweet nectar, which we will then offer in a very special feeder created appositely for our colourful friends.

Butterfly nectar recipe
To make butterfly nectar mix 4 parts water with 1 part sugar, or 9 parts water with 1 part honey. Boil until the sugar/honey has completely dissolved.
Let it cool.

It is important to remember that butterflies taste with their feet. Therefore, when we offer nectar, we need to ensure that it won't leave the butterfly drenched in sticky fluid. The easiest way to do this is by using a feeder.

There are many ways to create butterfly feeders – these are my favourite two, which are super fun and easy to make with children. Feel free to use your creativity and whatever materials you have at home to craft something completely unique!

MAKE IT WITH US!
WATCH THE VIDEO OF HOW
WE MAKE BUTTERFLY
FEEDERS

TERRACOTTA POT FEEDER

Butterfly feeders made from terracotta pots are easy to create, inexpensive and it's a great way to upcycle old pots. Children love decorating them, and they always look great in the garden!

Things to gather:

- a terracotta saucer or wide shallow bowl
- river rocks, decorative pebbles
- paint, fabric flowers, other natural decorative elements (optional)

Directions. Find an old, shallow terracotta bowl or a wide saucer. Clean it and paint it in bright colours; butterflies are particularly attracted to orange, yellow, purple, and pink.

Once dry, add some small pebbles for the butterflies to land upon, allowing them to stay dry while drinking. This is essential to protect their feet and wings. Fill with butterfly nectar and place it on the ground, near your flower beds.

Another beautiful feeder can be made with a small terracotta pot and saucer (choose a saucer that is slightly larger than the base of the pot).
Follow these steps:

- Flip the pot upside down, so that it acts as a base, and glue the saucer on top of it.
- Decorate the feeder by adding pebbles, beads, or fresh flowers. This is optional, but looks so pretty!
- Fill the feeder with butterfly nectar, and remember to replace the solution every two to three days.

GLASS BOTTLE FEEDER

Find a beautiful old bottle for this craft. Young children might need assistance with the knots.

Things to gather:
- a glass bottle
- a sponge
- twine or string

Directions. Prepare two pieces of string or twine, each about 1 metre long. Wrap each string around the neck of the bottle and secure them with double knots, facing each other. Now you'll have four bits of string extending from the bottle. Criss-cross them and tie a double knot about halfway up the bottle. This step will create a simple macrame-style structure to hold your bottle securely.

Repeat the previous step once more to reinforce the structure, giving your butterfly feeder stability.

Get creative and decorate the bottle with faux flowers in bright colours, beads, or any other decorative elements you like. Fill the bottle with butterfly nectar.

Cut a strip of sponge and carefully push it through the neck of the bottle, leaving about 1-2 cm poking out. You want to ensure that the sponge fits snugly into the opening.

Now hang the feeder upside down from a sturdy tree branch, allowing the nectar to slowly release. Enjoy the mesmerising sight of butterflies as they visit your feeder and bring life to your garden.

Remember to refill the bottle and replace the sponge as needed.

Observe the butterflies as they come and go, enjoying the delicious treats provided.
Are you able to identify any species? It might be a fun challenge to find a nature guide featuring images of butterflies native to your area and see how many you can spot.

GROW HOST PLANTS

Before they can become gorgeous, winged insects, butterflies are first slow, lumbering caterpillars that spend their days munching on leaves. If you want to attract butterflies to your garden, consider supporting their complete lifecycle by planting caterpillar host plants.

Adult butterflies lay their eggs on the underside of leaves, but only on plants that are suitable food sources for their hungry larvae. The host plants that butterflies choose for their young are very specific – for example, monarch butterflies will only use milkweed, while caterpillars of the imperial blue butterfly are only found on wattles.

Do some research – ask your local plant nursery, or check the environmental resources provided by your council - and grow some host plants in your garden.

Imagine being able to observe the metamorphosis and all the stages of a butterfly's life cycle – from egg to larva to pupa to butterfly – in your own backyard. It's a fascinating and awe-inspiring miracle of nature!

While each butterfly species will have its own preferences, most are attracted to blooms that are white, pink, purple, red, yellow, and orange. Flowers with blue or green tones are generally the least liked by butterflies.

NOVEMBER

THE GROUNDING ENERGY OF ROCKS

November is a month of luscious colours. Many parts of our country are still covered with wildflowers: meadows of daisies, orchids dotting the forest path, desert peas emerging from the driest of landscapes. Cities are blanketed in swathes of light-purple jacaranda petals.

November also marks the beginning of the wet season in the tropical north of Australia, bringing heavy rains, high humidity and fierce storms. The colours of the rainforest are at their brightest and the waterfalls are full and spectacular. The Great Barrier Reef comes alive with the annual coral spawning.

As spring transitions to summer, we sense a renewed feeling of lightness growing within us. But before we dive into the vibrant expansiveness of summer life, we pause for a moment to find our centre, using the grounding energy of natural rocks.

EARTH MAGIC

EVERYBODY NEEDS A ROCK

From the depths of the Earth's crust to the surface, shaped over millennia by the forces of nature, rocks carry the tales of our planet's transformations.

Scattered across landscapes, from mountains to riverbeds, carved by water and wind – sometimes hiding, waiting to be uncovered by curious eyes. Through the tactile experience of feeling rocks' textures, observing their colours, and tracing their patterns, we can connect with the Earth's past and present.

Not surprisingly, rocks carry grounding energy; even just holding them in the palm of our hands can help us feel calm and centred.

A GROUNDING PRACTICE

Have you ever been 'called' by a rock – maybe as you strolled on a quiet beach, or climbed through pristine mountains? There is usually something we feel attracted to – its shape, colour, or smooth texture. As you roll it gently in the palm of your hand, its solid presence serves as a conduit to the grounding energy that flows through our planet.

Close your eyes, let your fingers explore its surface, and let its weight anchor you to the present moment. Place the rock in a spot where it can receive the Sun's embrace, then hold it. Feel the heat flowing into your body, and the connection between you, the Earth and the Sun.

Simple nature connection practices, such as the one just described, hold an incredible power to bring us back to the present moment, and into our centre.

FULL MOON

GO FOR A FULL MOON WALK

Ready for an adventure? Go for a family night walk beneath the Moon's radiant glow. You don't need to venture too far; even a short stroll along your street or around the backyard can be a magical experience for your children.

Notice the subtle changes that the full moon brings to the surroundings – how everything is bathed in a gentle light. Listen for sounds of the natural world responding to this magnificent cosmic event.

In the Northern Hemisphere, the November full moon goes by the name "Beaver moon", as this is the time when beavers begin to build their shelters in preparation for the cold season. Meanwhile, in the Southern Hemisphere, where summer is on the horizon, we refer to this moon as the "Corn moon", "Milk moon", or "Flower moon".

Look at the Moon this month – which one of these names describes it better for you?

FULL MOON MAGIC POTION

In some old folk traditions the Moon is considered the guardian witch of planet Earth. So this is the time to get your cauldron out (or a bowl) and create your very own full moon elixir.

Things to gather:

- fresh rosemary, rose petals, plus any other herbs and flowers available
- water
- a bowl

Directions. Mix the fresh rosemary, rose petals and water into a bowl. Let your child play with it – stirring, mixing, grinding, pounding... Allow the plants to infuse the water, then transfer into a spray bottle.

Rosemary is renowned for its protective qualities and its ability to ward off bad dreams, while rose is known to nurture love, grace and joy. Use as room mist or spray over bed linens to bring serenity to your days and nights.

IN THE KITCHEN

LET'S MAKE STONE SOUP

Remember the story Stone Soup? It's a timeless tale that teaches us about the power of collaboration, generosity, and community. The clever hungry travellers in the story use their ingenuity to bring people together and create a delicious meal out of seemingly nothing. It's a beautiful reminder that when we share and work together, we can achieve wonderful things.

If you have a copy of this book read it with your child. There are many versions of the story, but my personal favourite is the one by Heather Forest.
And now, let's make stone soup together!

Ingredients:

- 1 large, clean stone
  (for storytelling purposes)
- 1 tbsp olive oil
- 1 onion, chopped
- 2 carrots, peeled and sliced
- 2 celery stalks, chopped
- 2 cloves garlic, minced
- 4 cups vegetable or chicken broth
- 1 potato, diced
- 1 turnip
- 1 cup of your favourite mixed vegetables
  (peas, corn, green beans)
- 1 cup of rice (optional)
- salt and pepper to taste
- fresh herbs (such as thyme, parsley)
- a dash of kindness

Directions

Set the scene – Begin by sharing the story of Stone Soup with your children. Show them the clean stone and explain how it's a special ingredient that adds magic to the soup.

Prepare the stone – Wash the stone thoroughly and set it aside. This step is mostly for fun and storytelling.

Sauté the aromatics – Add the olive oil into a large pot over medium heat. Add the chopped onion, sliced carrots, and chopped celery. Sauté until the vegetables start to soften and the onions turn translucent.

Add the flavour – Stir in the minced garlic and cook for another minute until fragrant.

The stone's entry – Dramatically add the clean stone to the pot, just like in the story. Explain that the stone adds a special touch to the soup.

Simmer and add goodness – Pour in the vegetable or chicken broth. Add the diced potato and mixed vegetables to the pot. If using, add rice or other grains. Season with salt and pepper to taste.

Cooking together – Let the soup simmer over low heat for about 20-25 minutes, until the vegetables are tender and the flavours mix together. As the soup simmers, you can encourage children to share their thoughts about the story, or create their own version, fostering a sense of togetherness.

Remove the stone – Just like in the story, "discover" the stone and remove it from the pot. It has done its job of adding a hint of magic to the soup!

Taste and adjust – Have the children taste the soup and discuss the flavours. You can also encourage them to suggest any seasonings they'd like to add.

Serve with a dash of kindness – Ladle the warm stone soup into bowls. Before serving, remind children about the most important ingredient – kindness.

Garnish and enjoy – Sprinkle fresh herbs over each bowl for a burst of colour and flavour. Enjoy your stone soup together.

This stone soup recipe is not just about the ingredients; it's about the joy of coming together, sharing stories, and nurturing a sense of togetherness.
Enjoy the magic you've created with each spoonful!

NATURE PLAY

PLAYING WITH STONES

Playing with rocks and stones engages the senses and our imagination, allowing us to tell stories or create unique patterns. By collecting, stacking, or crafting with rocks, children engage with nature in a tangible manner.

Let's explore different ways in which we can play and create with them!

GATHERING

Step outside and begin your stone-hunting adventure! There are plenty of exciting places where you can discover natural stones: the beach, a trail, a river, or a park. Take a small basket or a bucket to help your child carry these newly found treasures.

Remember to collect responsibly and consider returning the stones after playtime.

Observations
Together, look at the rocks you collected. Do they sparkle? Are they colourful? Are they smooth or rough? Do they look like crystals or precious stones? How would you best describe them? You can use this opportunity to introduce new vocabulary.

SORTING

Provide containers or empty egg cartons for children to explore a rock sorting activity. Encourage them to organise their rock collection according to various characteristics, such as size, shape, colour, texture, weight, or even how well they roll.

Older children can create labels or drawings for each category, enhancing their organisation and cognitive skills through playful exploration.

CRITTER FRIENDS

Using paint and permanent markers, turn your rocks into little bugs, friendly animals, magical creatures, cheeky monsters, or simply draw faces on it – happy, sad, angry, surprised... Which one are you today?

Once the rocks are dry, provide children with a bin or bowl filled with various natural treasures like leaves, twigs, pebbles, and flowers. Encourage them to use these natural materials to construct a cosy hideout, a miniature home, or a special play space for their newly created rock creature friends.

This imaginative activity blends art, nature, and storytelling, sparking endless possibilities for creative play.

SPIRIT ANIMAL STONES

Ask your child to identify an animal that holds special significance to them – their spirit animal. Explain that these creatures embody qualities that we admire and aspire to cultivate within ourselves. They can guide us and offer protection.

Using stones as a canvas, ask them to inscribe markings that encapsulate the essence of their chosen spirit animals – maybe it is bravery, compassion, wisdom, curiosity, or loyalty.

Sew a small bag out a piece of canvas or felt to hold your spirit animal stone close. These sacred animal stones can become powerful tools. In times of need, encourage children to seek guidance and strength from their animal allies – to summon courage, provide insight, or navigate challenges.

ROCK BATH

Set up a bowl of soapy water and provide tools such as sponges, washcloths, or even an old toothbrush. Encourage children to give their collected rocks a good scrub. Observe the transformation as the rocks become wet compared to when they are dry. It is so fascinating to see how colours and patterns change in the water, often becoming more vibrant.

This activity offers a hands-on way to explore the natural beauty of rocks while engaging in sensory play.

LOOSE PARTS PLAY

Young children can play with stones and rocks for hours and hours! Place the rocks in your play area with two or more small baskets. Watch your child moving them in and out, stacking them, carrying baskets around, using them as food in the mud kitchen, tables and chairs for the fairies... The possibilities are endless!

CREATING SHAPES

Using a piece of string or sidewalk chalk, create the outline of a spiral, circle, or any other shape. Alternatively, you can draw a line in the dirt or sand using a stick or your finger.

Encourage your child to follow the outline you've created as they carefully place stones along its path or let them create their own shape.

ROCK EXCAVATION

Introduce your child to the fascinating world of geology by simulating the process of discovering special rocks. Provide them with simple tools like a stick and a paintbrush, which mimic the techniques used by geologists.

Things to gather:

- 1 cup of flour
- 1 cup of used coffee grounds
- 1/2 a cup of salt
- 1/4 cup sand
- 3/4 cup water

Directions. Mix all dry ingredients in a bowl. Slowly add water and knead mixture until it holds together. Take a handful of dough and flatten it out, placing a special stone or inexpensive crystal in the middle. Add more mixture and form an egg/stone shape. Let the mixture air dry for 2-4 days or until hard.

Now it comes the fun part! Invite children to delicately uncover and extract rocks from the earth, mimicking the careful excavation process of geologists. They can break open the treasure stones with their hands, with a larger rock or using a small hammer.

Alternatively, bury some rocks from your collection in the dirt or sand, prompting the kids to embark on an excavation adventure.

As they uncover each rock, encourage them to observe its texture, shape, and colour, fostering an understanding of how rocks are hidden treasures waiting to be unearthed.

Tossing rocks is such a simple play activity for kids to do outdoors in nature, and yet it is so entertaining.

MINDFULNESS

WORLD KINDNESS DAY

Here's an invitation to bring more kindness into our lives. World Kindness Day, on November 13th is a beautiful celebration reminding us all that kindness should be the norm in our daily life – not the exception. Use this special day as an opportunity to mindfully build a new routine which includes intentional moments of kindness, laughter and delight every day.

By sharing kindness and making these actions intentional, children learn the profound impact they can have on others. They learn about reciprocity and the ripple effect – how one kind action can inspire more acts of kindness, creating a chain reaction of positivity.

Here are some mindful activities that will prompt a conversation with your child about kindness. Start from here and see where it leads you... be prepared to be amazed!

KINDNESS ROCKS

One message at just the right moment can change someone's entire day, outlook, life. That's how powerful our words can be!

A beautiful practice is to write positive messages and leave them in random places for others to find and read. You can use post-it notes but since we will be playing with rocks this month, why not use some from your collection? Let's gather a few supplies and get painting.

Things to gather:

- a selection of smooth rocks
- paintbrushes
- acrylic paints or pens

Directions. Write a positive, uplifting message on your rock. Personalise it with your unique touch! Have fun hiding these rocks around your house, neighbourhood or park, or maybe create a kindness rocks garden at your school.

Extensions.
Brainstorm ideas of things you could do to spread kindness. Begin with family members and close friends, then extend the circle of kindness to neighbours, your community, and even strangers. Can you think of any ways to show kindness to the natural world? Consider the needs of the animals, birds, or insects inhabiting your environment at this moment, and how you could help them. Do they need water, food, shelter?

For more ideas and inspiration visit the Random Acts of Kindness Foundation website and sign up to become a RAKtivist!

DECEMBER

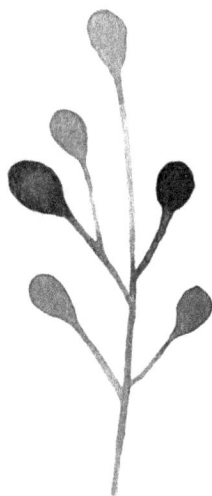

WELCOME SUMMER

Gliders, flying foxes, and rainbow lorikeets are feasting on the abundance of pink and red bloodwood flowers. Koalas are breeding, and the melodic calls of cicadas fill the air. As summer takes hold, gum trees shed their bark, and snakes gracefully shed their skin. Streets are adorned with blooming poinciana trees, showcasing a luscious display of flamboyant red flowers. Welcome, summer.

The Earth rejoices in its fertility and bounty. The Sun radiates brightly, its life-giving power in full glory, culminating on the special day known as Midsummer. This ancient celebration marks the summer solstice, where the Sun reaches its highest position in the sky, giving us the longest day of the year.

Midsummer is a time of magic – a time when fairies mingle with humans, trees whisper secrets, and dreams can come true. It is a time when herbs and flowers reach the peak of their healing properties, and were traditionally gathered on this auspicious day for use in medicine and spells.

This month we celebrate light, and life.

EARTH MAGIC

DANDELIONS

With my tiny yellow gold petals, I look a lot like the Sun. I am bright and cheerful, and my gentle aroma has the power to warm your soul. As the first rays of sunshine grace the day I wake up, but like a weary traveller, I prefer to rest at night.

As I grow old, I turn into a delicate white full moon. Pick me up, and with a gentle blow – whoof – silently make a wish. Watch me as I scatter into a galaxy of stars – these are my seeds, ready to embark on their journey. Carried by the breeze, they will travel far and wide, finding new roots in the welcoming embrace of the Earth.

I am the dandelion. My flowers are a delectable feast for honeybees, butterflies, and moths. Every single petal – and trust me, I have many! Can you count them? – brims with delicious nectar and precious pollen.

But I am more than a delightful treat for nature's creatures; I bring gifts of healing and nourishment to you, too, my sweet child. My flowers will soothe your skin when it's red and itchy.

Bring me into your home – I will fill your space with happiness and joy, and remind you of how brave your heart can be.

In French, I am known as *dent-de-lion*, which means lion's tooth.

I can be gentle and kind, strong and courageous at the same time. And so can you, my dear one.

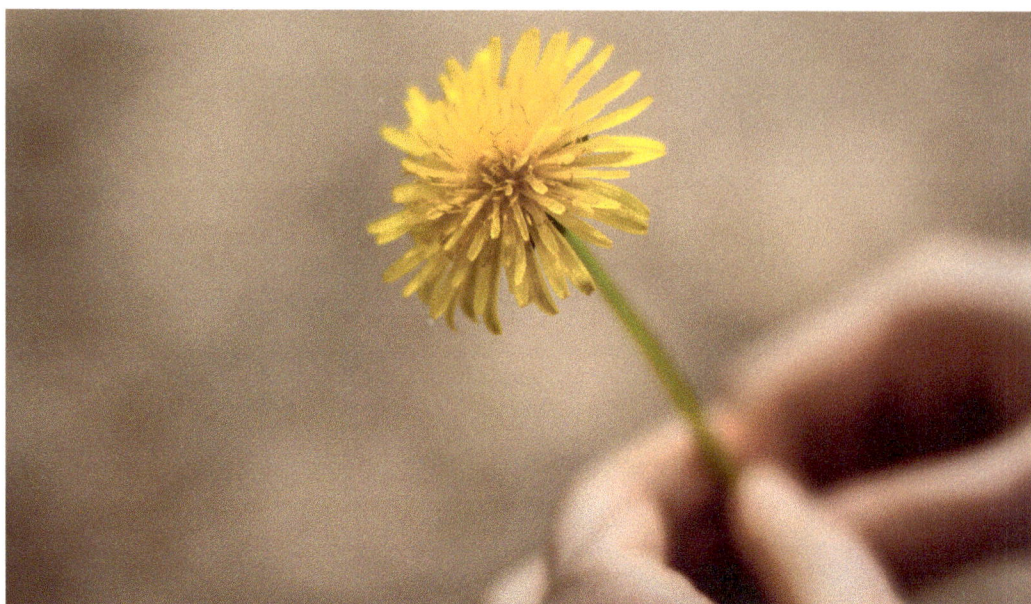

GATHERING

On a sunny morning, venture outdoors to collect dandelions basking in the warmth of the Sun. Look for open flowers, take some time to observe their beauty.

When picking wildflowers, always remember the golden rule: **I pick one for me, leave five for the bees.**

GET JOURNALING

Dandelions have an extraordinary connection with the Sun! They joyfully wake up in the morning, stretching their vibrant petals to soak up the Sun's warm rays. However, during the night or on rainy days, they close up, seeking rest and protection.

Capture the magic of these sun-loving blooms in your nature journal. Let your creativity flow as you illustrate the enchanting dandelions in all their splendour.

Some people believe that dandelions are the only flowers that, at various stages of their life cycle, symbolically represent the Sun, the Moon, and stars. Can you illustrate these stages?

Dandelions have so many petals... counting them can be quite a task! The head contains between 100 and 300 tiny florets (individual flowers). So each petal represents a single flower. Beneath the bright golden yellow head, five tiny petals sit above a tube brimming with an abundance of sweet nectar.

Can you find it?

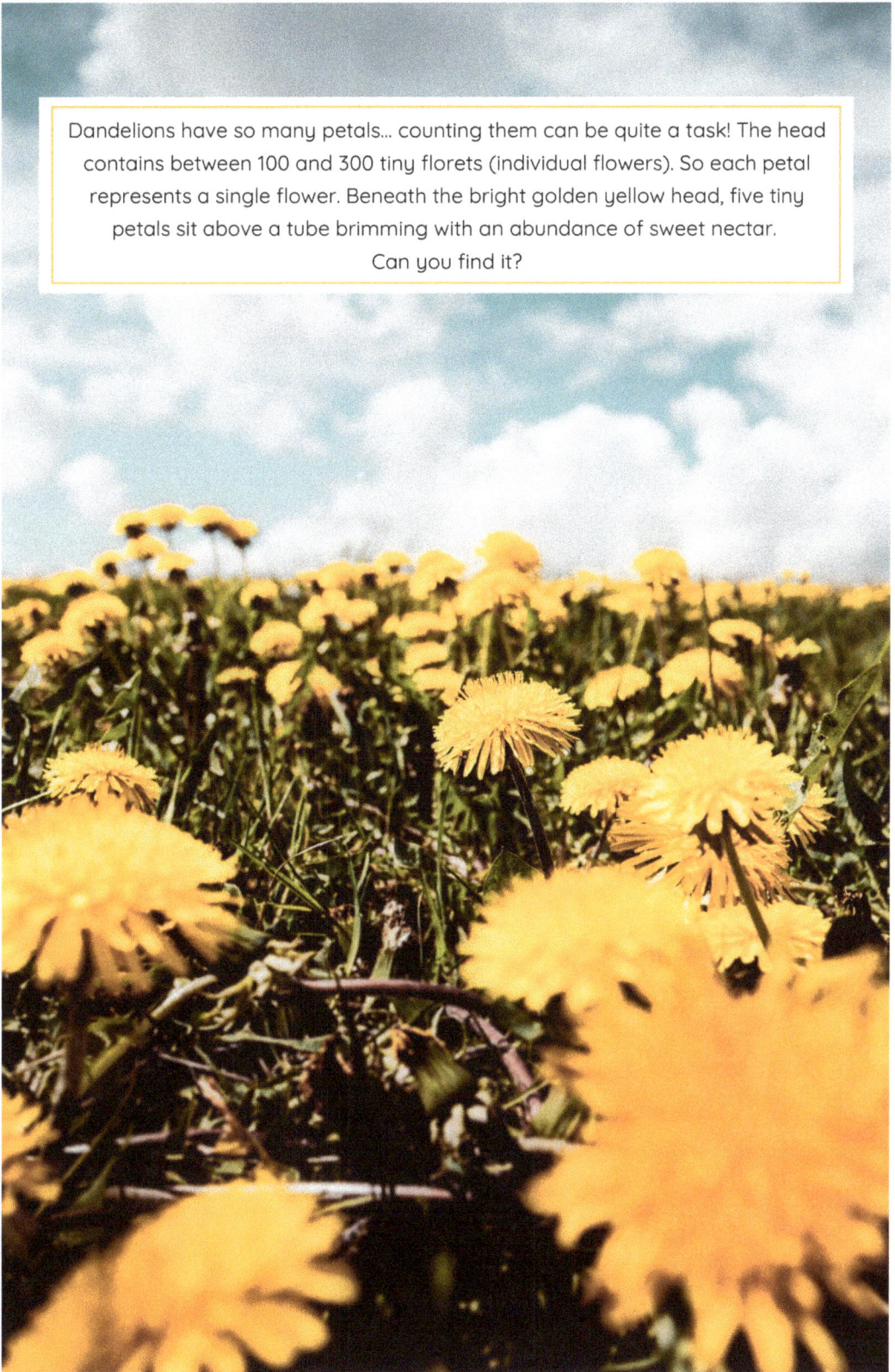

DANDELION MEDICINAL OIL

Dandelion oil smells like summertime, and it's so simple to make. Beyond its delightful aroma, this oil is perfect to nourish and revitalise dry skin, and can be used to treat minor cuts, scrapes, bug bites and skin irritations.

Make it part of your natural first aid kit at home, and fill a small roller bottle to keep in your purse and/or in your child's backpack.

Things to gather:

- freshly picked dandelion blossoms (ensure they haven't come into contact with any harmful chemicals)
- oil of choice – olive, almond, apricot, fractionated coconut or jojoba oil are all wonderful options
- a clean jar
- muslin cloth

Directions. Gently rinse or brush the flowers to eliminate any lingering insects. Separate the flower heads from their stems and lay them out on paper towels. Keep in a sunny location for several hours in order to remove excess moisture.

Once the flowers are dry, invite your little helper to pluck the petals and place them gently into the clean jar.

Fill approximately half of the jar's volume with dandelion petals, leaving the remaining space for the oil. Use a piece of muslin cloth secured by a rubber band to cover the jar's opening. Position the jar in a dark cupboard for up to two weeks, allowing the oil to infuse.

After this time you can strain the blossoms and transfer the oil into a clean jar. It is now ready to use!

Optional. Feel free to add 10-20 drops of your favourite essential oil.

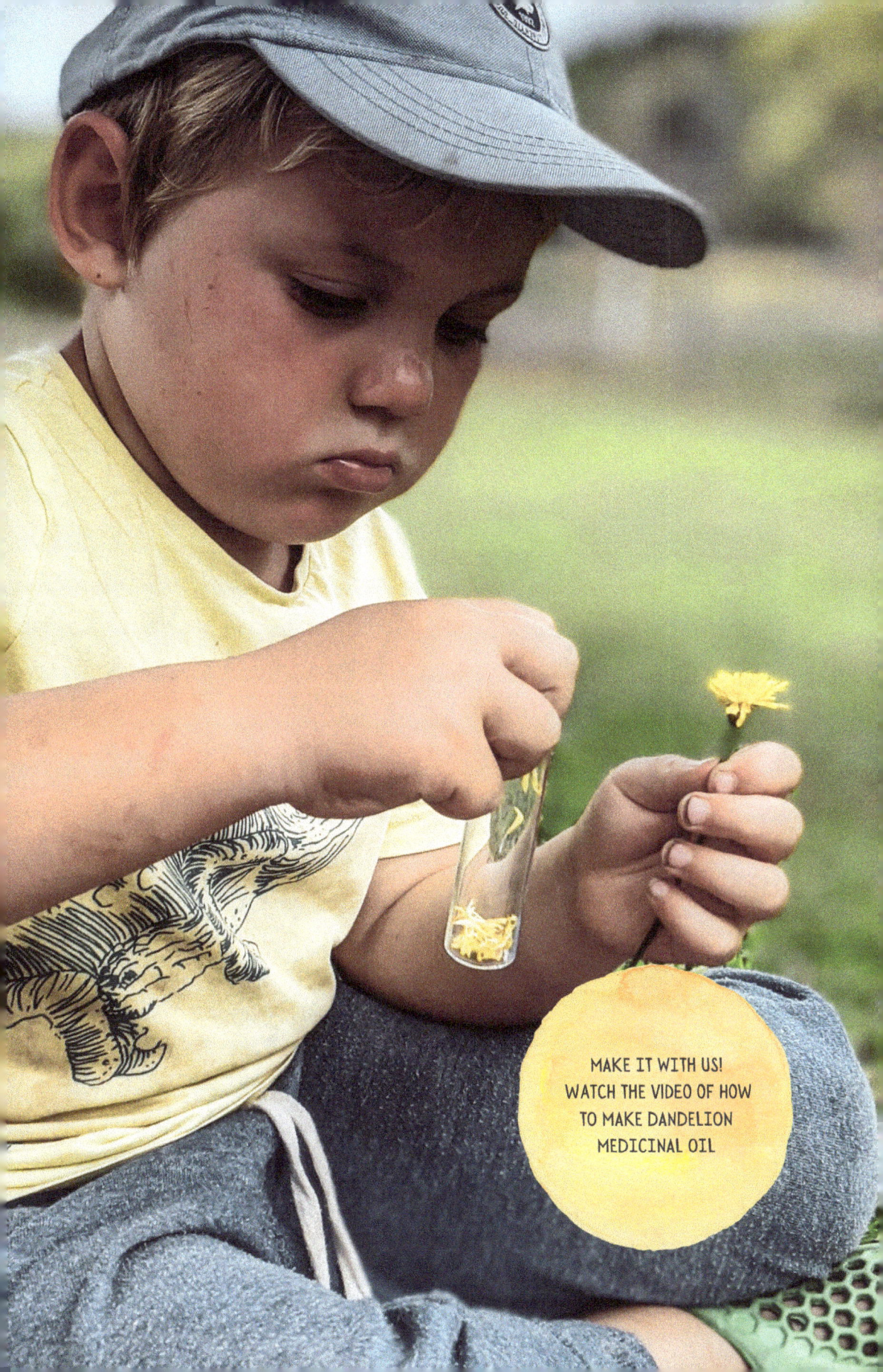

MAKE IT WITH US!
WATCH THE VIDEO OF HOW
TO MAKE DANDELION
MEDICINAL OIL

SUMMER SOLSTICE MAGIC

"On Midsummer we eat and dance with abandon, leaving all worries behind.
The Sun never sets and there are flowers everywhere."

The summer solstice, also referred to as Midsummer, marks the apex of the Sun's
potency and the longest day of the year.

Our European ancestors used to celebrate midsummer with bonfires and dancing, and
by gathering plants and herbs. They believed that, on this day, plants reached the peak
of their healing powers as they fully absorbed the Sun's life force.

St. John's Wort, rosemary, vervain, hyssop, fern, mullein, basil, lavender, thyme,
fennel, and wormwood were gathered for healing and magic. Rose, wild daisy,
marigold, cornflower and calendula were used to attract beauty and love, their petals
scattered in water for love charms.

In Bohemia, girls wore chaplets of mugwort while dancing around the Midsummer
bonfire. In Italy people washed their faces in bowls of water containing flowers, rose
petals and herbs.

What will be your own Midsummer ritual? Perhaps a sun-kissed picnic with friends?
An evening by the seashore? Or maybe sharing music and stories with friends around
a flickering campfire?

MAGIC HERBS POUCH

Become a green witch for a day! If using fresh flowers and herbs, ensure they are completely dry before adding to your pouch.

Things to gather:

- fresh or dried flowers, such as rosemary, lavender, mugwort, or calendula
- a drawstring pouch for dried flowers, or natural string to keep fresh herbs together

Directions. Gather, bundle and enjoy! Offering a bunch of herbs on Midsummer day makes a very special gift.

FULL MOON

DANDELION HONEY

The December full moon is known as the Strawberry or Honey moon – a moon with an amber glow, like the honey our beloved bees are diligently producing.

Infusing honey with medicinal flowers is ancient practice – not only it tastes delicious, it's also a great natural remedy for coughs, colds, and sore throats.

Things to gather:

- fresh dandelion flowers
- raw honey
- a clean jar

Directions. Collect a small bunch of fully opened dandelions, ensuring they are sourced from an area that hasn't been sprayed with chemicals.

Arrange the flowers on a tray and leave them in the full sun for an hour or more, allowing all the moisture to evaporate. Once they are ready, invite your child to help you pluck the petals and place them into the clean jar.

Fill about a quarter of the jar with dandelion petals, then pour in the honey to top it off. Give it a good stir, and store it in a dark cupboard for about four weeks to allow the infusion to take place.

After this time, you can choose to strain off the petals or leave them in. Your delicious dandelion-infused honey is ready to eat! Drizzle some on your morning toast or porridge, or take a spoonful straight on those days when your soul needs a little bit of extra sunshine.

It also makes a beautiful holiday gift.

IN THE KITCHEN

HAPPY SUMMER TEA

Enjoy this delicious herbal tea served cold on ice, on warm summer days.

Ingredients:

- dried chamomile flowers
- dried lavender flowers
- dried or fresh mint leaves
- juice of one lemon, plus one to slice
- dandelion infused honey
- floral ice cubes (optional)

Method. Using a tea infuser, add 2 tbsp of the dried flowers and few mint leaves, to 4 cups of freshly boiled water. Allow to steep for 5-10 minutes. Stir in the lemon juice, add the lemon slices and 1 tbsp of dandelion infused honey (or more, according to taste). Allow to cool, transfer to pitcher, and refrigerate.

Serve over ice and enjoy!

Optional. To make floral ice cubes simply add the prettiest, brightest edible flowers to an ice tray, fill with water and freeze.

NATURE PLAY

MAKE A DANDELION POUCH

Dandelions smile with the Sun! Capture their beauty in a simple, yet lovely pouch, perfect for holding your child's most precious treasures.

Things to gather:

- watercolour, acrylic or earth paint
- calico drawstring bags
- a piece of cardboard
- one or two dandelions to use as stamps

Directions. To begin, cut a piece of cardboard to fit inside the drawstring bag, ensuring the paint won't seep through to the other side.

Pick a dandelions and dip its flower head into the paint, ensuring it's thoroughly coated. Use it as a stamp to decorate your drawstring bag with the beautiful imprints of these sunny flowers.

WILDFLOWER PLAYDOUGH

Warm and fresh playdough combined with essential oils and the enchanting scents of herbs and flowers forms the perfect tactile canvas for little hands to roll, pinch, stack, flatten, and mould.

This wonderful wildflower playdough offers not just sensory joy but also a magical connection to nature's scents and textures. As you create and explore, remember the precious gift of sharing – pass on this sensory wonder to another curious young heart or keep it nestled in your child's hands for hours of imaginative play.

Things to gather:

- 1 cup flour
- 1/2 a cup salt
- 2 tsp cream of tartar
- 1 tbsp olive oil
- 1 cup boiling water
- 1/2 tsp ground turmeric (optional)
- a handful of dried or fresh flowers and herbs (dandelions, violets, borage, lavender, rosemary)
- lavender essential oil (optional)

Directions. Begin by adding the turmeric to the hot the water, increasing the quantity for a deeper colour, if desired. Stir the mixture thoroughly.

Combine the flour, salt, and cream of tartar in a bowl. Pour the olive oil and the coloured water into the mixture, stirring as you go. Add the petals and herbs to your creation, giving it a gentle mix. Knead for about a minute.

If the mixture seems sticky, add more flour. If too dry, lightly rub a few drops of oil onto your hands and continue kneading until the dough has a soft, smooth consistency. Shape into a ball and allow it to cool completely. Preserve it in an airtight container within the refrigerator.

MIDSUMMER MAGIC WAND

I love making magic wands, in fact I make one at the beginning of each season and use it to keep all my seasonal nature treasures together. But the Midsummer wand is a special one... I'll go as far as to add some crystals and precious amulets to it to symbolise the magic of this time of year.

Things to gather:

- a special stick
- flowers, leaves, feathers, natural string, cones and seedpods a small crystal (optional)

Directions. Arrange all your nature treasures items around the stick and secure with string.

Banksia cones are associated with the Sun, and their Noongar name 'birytch' is connected to the word for daylight ('biryt'), due to their uses related to fire. I think including either a banksia flower or cone would make a wonderful addition to this wand!

PLANT IDENTIFICATION CARDS

Help children identify magical herbs and plants growing in your garden using these printable cards.

ROSEMARY

DANDELION

CHAMOMILE

LAVENDER

THYME

CALENDULA

MINDFULNESS

THE WISE DANDELION

The ephemeral life of the dandelion is a perfect reminder that everything is constantly changing – in our minds, in our bodies and in the world around us. This is called impermanence.

Consider for a moment the life cycle of this extraordinary plant: Its seeds floating far from home, taking root, blossoming in a quick burst of colour only to be floating once again. Tireless, resilient, yet ever so graceful the wise dandelion knows that the wind of change comes, it is time to let go.

It may not always be in bloom, but the continuous cycle of change means that sunny days are never too far away.

CONCLUSION

And so we have come to the end of our year together. The Earth moved slowly through its journey around the Sun, while we lived in the round of the seasons, feeling held in nature's encircling love.

Perhaps along this journey, you may have discovered certain activities, recipes, or practices that resonated deeply with you. I invite you to revisit them with your child year after year. Children delight in the comfort of repetition, and each year brings fresh opportunities to explore further, wider, and deeper.

I hope this book will become a cherished keepsake in your family – filled with photographs, dried leaves and flowers, notes and drawings that will remind you of the countless adventures you've had together and all those that are yet to come.

May it accompany you and your child on this ever-unfolding journey of love and discovery, as you continue to grow, *together*, with nature.

RESOURCES

Our online resource page provides downloadable files that can be printed and used for personal use (not for resale).

Please visit www.bigscrubnatureplay.com/resources to download your free resources. On our website you will also find step-by-step videos guiding you through some of the crafts and activities in this book.

REFERENCED WORKS

[1] Twomey, A. (1995). Opening speech at the 1995 Tea Tree Oil National Conference - from folklore to fact. All about tea tree oil. https://teatree.org.au/teatree_about.php

[2] Carroll, S. (2023). Ochre is of the Earth. Bangarra Dance Theatre Knowledge Ground. https://bangarra-knowledgeground.com.au/productions/ochres/ochre-is-of-the-earth

[3] Malaguzzi, L. (2022). 100 languages (L. Gandini trans). Reggio Emelia Approach. https://www.reggiochildren.it/en/reggio-emilia-approach/100-linguaggi-en/

[4] Peters, E. (1977). In conversation with Joseph "Bearwalker" Wilson. American neopaganism, part 3: Past, present, and future. https://www.patheos.com/blogs/allergicpagan/2012/05/08/american-neopaganism-part-3-past-present-and-future/

[5] Hamacher, D. (Ed.) (2012). The origin of the Moon. Australian Indigenous Astronomy. https://aboriginalastronomy.blogspot.com/2012/01/origin-of-moon.html

[6] Moran, C. (2004). Talk softly, listen well. Southern Cross University Press.

7 Starchild, A learning centre for young astronomers. https://starchild.gsfc.nasa.gov/docs/StarChild/StarChild.html

THANK YOUS

My deepest gratitude goes to my whole family and particularly to my husband Luca - my partner in life and adventure. Thank you for believing in me. This book would not exist without you.

A heart-felt thank you to my editor, Wallea Eaglehawk, for her guidance and support, and to Sarah Deck, for offering her time, insight and expertise so generously. Thank you to David Sewell McCann for sharing his vast knowledge and passion on restorative storytelling with me, and encouraging me to write the stories in this book, and many more.

I am so blessed to be surrounded by some pretty amazing human beings and friends who, at various stages, have offered advice, encouragement, playdates for my children and a shoulder to cry on. A special thanks goes to Julie and Cath, who in addition to their unwavering support, gracefully offered their time to help me edit the final version of this book.

Thank you to all the children and families I have spent time with in nature over the years, and who continue to support my work through Big Scrub Nature Play. You have inspired this book.

To all my teachers along the way – the plants and the animals, the trees and the birds. To this deeply magical land I call home. Thank you.

www.ingramcontent.com/pod-product-compliance
Lightning Source LLC
Chambersburg PA
CBHW060756150426
42811CB00058B/1425